Truthful Light

Reflections of God Moments: Book 12

Dedication

I dedicate this book to all my friends who have stood beside me being the light through the dark places when I felt alone. Thank you for sharing your truthful light when the darkness threatened to overwhelm my life. Vergie & Charles, Rhonda & Jeremy, Kelley & Randy, Janice & Carlos, Jeanine, Meredith, Debbie, Athene and so many more. I cannot begin to list all of you who continue to carry your truthful light into this darkened world...you have blessed me and shined the light into dark places so we knew we did not walk alone.

Truthful Light
Reflections of God Moments Book 12
copyright © 2025

Written by: Donesa Walker
Design by: Will Baten
Edited by: Kelley Inderman

Contents

Plain Truth!....................................5

The Best!....................................7

Royal Authority!....................................9

Mine Forever!....................................11

Constant Calling!....................................13

Coming Day!....................................15

Words Remembered!....................................17

Steady Stream!....................................19

God Breathed!....................................21

Serious Searching!....................................23

Real Surprise!....................................25

Image Making!....................................27

Supple Moves!....................................29

Fits & Starts!....................................31

Recognizing Him!....................................33

Prevailing Purpose!....................................35

Deep Spirited!....................................37

God's Terms!....................................39

Flowing Down!....................................41

The Focus!....................................43

God Conviction!....................................45

Particular Please!....................................47

Healed Inside!....................................49

Life-Light!....................................51

Back Right!....................................53

Grace Shower!....................................55

Recover Life!....................................57

Full Measure!....................................59

The Best!....................................61

Trustworthy!....................................63

God Absorbed!....................................65

Listening Truth!....................................67

Redoubled Effort!....................................69

Perfect Love!....................................71

Proper Behavior!....................................73

Testing Challenge!....................................75

Wordless Sighs!....................................77

Happy Life!....................................79

Reach Out!....................................81

Right Here!....................................83

Wholly Mature!....................................85

Catch His Breath!....................................87

Urgent Job!....................................89

Strong Warrior!....................................91

Talking Praise!....................................93

God Container!....................................95

Shared Life!....................................97

Combined Character!....................................99

God Measure!....................................101

Small Potatoes!....................................103

Living One!....................................105

Praise Shaped!....................................107

Don't Panic!....................................109

First Love!....................................111

Attempt the Impossible!....................................113

Last Words!....................................115

Just then he looked up and saw the rich people dropping offerings in the collection plate. Then he saw a poor widow put in two pennies. He said, "The plain truth is that this widow has given by far the largest offering today. All these others made offerings that they'll never miss; she gave extravagantly what she couldn't afford—she gave her all!"

Luke 21: 1-4

Plain Truth!

Giving all is the ultimate gift that Christ gave for us! As Jesus looked at the givers in the Temple, He saw the widow who gave less than all others but in terms of ability to give, she had given more because she gave all that she had. We often get caught up in our own thoughts, feelings and importance so that we give little of ourselves but expect much. We are so invested in our own wants and desires that we fail to recognize that we are not so generous with our all to Christ but continue to guard a portion for ourselves. What is all that God desires from us? It is our first. Our first in all is the best. Our first in attendance, attention and time. I admit that today was a day that my first was stolen rather than held for the One who gave all. Distractions abounded and the time got away from me and so the first of my day has become the last in my day. The first is not about a time of day but a portion of the heart. My heart has longed all day for the time of fulfillment with God. I ached all day to spend the time with Him and purposed on my heart but everything kept getting in the way. I spoke words to Him throughout my day in haste and over meals and in driving and between clients but oh how I missed my special time with Him that had been stolen away. The plain truth is that in giving all to Him, we must sacrifice ourselves. We must give up whatever it is that holds our presence from His presence. We must make the time to be in His presence with fullness of joy and attention. We must not waste the time away that we could be with Him as time is a precious commodity that easily is frizzled away. Time is a precious gift and the one thing we can never get back. That gift of time spent with the King of Kings is sacred and worthy. He delights to spend time with us but looks to us to decide what pittance of time we will have for Him. Is He our first, our priority above all else or is the time with Him the things that get sacrificed on the altar of self? Our lives are demanding and time quickly passes. Sleep comes upon us and the hours are busy but time set apart for Him is never wasted. It is the gift that is priceless as we invest it with Him, He gives back to us tenfold. I encourage and implore you to invest your all. Don't squander your time upon that which fades and will not matter in eternity. Priority matters and His kingdom is built on sacrifice. What would you do to spend time in an audience with The King? Why are you waiting? He is softly and tenderly calling throughout our days and nights. He woos us to His presence for He desires His people. Give extravagantly of yourself, your heart, and your time because the King of Glory desires to spend the time with you. Don't give of that which you will not miss but give sacrificially as your very best and prioritize Him. He will wait on you as you wait on Him. The plain truth is that the largest offering you can give is your all as He gave His all for you and me. What gift would you give to your king? All He asks is for you to give your all! All to Jesus I surrender. All to Him I freely give. If I give all to Him in surrender, then all is His to use in blessing. If all you have is two pennies or two minutes, then give that all for that is the all He desires and is more worthy to Him than riches.

Get along among yourselves, each of you doing your part. Our counsel is that you warn the freeloaders to get a move on. Gently encourage the stragglers, and reach out for the exhausted, pulling them to their feet. Be patient with each person, attentive to individual needs. And be careful that when you get on each other's nerves you don't snap at each other. Look for the best in each other, and always do your best to bring it out.

1 Thessalonians 5:13b-15

The Best!

As I lay here in the wee hours of morning, I am praying for the marriage of my niece today. This scripture pops into my mind and heart that in marriage like any other relationship, giving the best of us is the challenge we must understand and undertake. To get along in life, we must each do our part. There are not many greater frustrations than when someone does not carry their own portion or part of a load. In Thessalonians, Paul counsels the church to tell the freeloaders to move it along, to either get it in gear or move out of the way. As I anticipate the drive ahead, I know it will require patience because invariably there are drivers who have a different agenda to getting to their location promptly. Sometimes the road rage many experience is because of unexpected things but I often see people who are holding up traffic because they are trying to look at situations rather than driving attentively. These folks cause frustration and more accidents as they try to look at what is causing the slowdown. In life, we are often in a hurry to arrive at a destination and we become impatient with others. Here in this passage, we are encouraged to be attentive to one another's needs and patient with each other. We all get on one another's nerves, but here we are cautioned to not snap at each other but to look for the best instead. I think that this is critical marriage advice and life counsel. Encourage each other. Reach out to one another when we are exhausted. Be patient with yourself and others. Be attentive to your fellow humans. Be careful of each other's feelings. Don't snap at them. Look for the best in each other and always do your best to bring it out. What better advice is there? If we implemented all these things, there wouldn't be issues in our world because we would truly be living as Jesus instructed us by putting others before ourselves.

Our lives are not our own. We belong to The Master of all creation. As we go about our day today and each day, we must reflect and remember this advice. Give your best. It doesn't matter what another does. You give your best and pray that others do the same. If we do all we can in service for Him, then what others do matters not. What is your best? Are you giving it to Him?

"Who would you rather be: the one who eats the dinner or the one who serves the dinner? You'd rather eat and be served, right? But I've taken my place among you as the one who serves. And you've stuck with me through thick and thin. Now I confer on you the royal authority my Father conferred on me so you can eat and drink at my table in my kingdom and be strengthened as you take up responsibilities among the congregations of God's people.

Luke 22: 27-30

Royal Authority!

"Now I confer on you the royal authority my Father conferred on me so you can eat and drink at my table in my kingdom and be strengthened as you take up responsibilities among the congregations of God's people."

As is such a tiny word but it is rich in meaning for it indicates an active stage of doing. We like to think of Jesus giving us God's authority as this is comforting and exciting. One little two letter word is important here though because it means that in order to have authority, we must first "take up responsibility". Responsibility means having a duty to deal with something or of having control over someone/something. Jesus conferred His authority over all things to those of us who take up responsibility only AS we do it. In other words, in the action of responsibility, we receive authority. In the act of service to Him, we receive authorization to act in His place. One does not occur without the other. Authorities get their power from those who confer the responsibility of such. A law enforcement officer acts on authority that is conferred on him/her by the people who authorize him to act. He/she loses that authority when they act outside the scope of provision that was given or conferred. Absolute authority is only given to One which God conferred upon Jesus as He was baptized by God Himself speaking from Heaven. When Jesus conferred His authority upon the disciples at the last supper, it was only given as they took up responsibilities. Our role/reward cycle is connected to the AS. The royal authority to dine with Jesus in eternity and to be strengthened in this life is only conferred upon us as we take up our roles that He has charged us with in life. Each of us has been given royal authority in and over different responsibilities and these adapt and change throughout our lives. When I married, I pledged to take on the responsibilities of a wife and helpmate. When I became a mother, I took on the responsibilities of Mother. So it is in each mission field of ministry that has been placed in our purview. Our performance of our spiritual responsibilities authorizes us to act on His behalf. He confers upon us the strength in the moment that we act-this is the AS. We want things to happen prior but just look at all the times of miraculous move in scripture. The water turned to wine as the servants acted. The Red Sea rolled back as the people stepped into it. The miracle occurs in the doing. What is the mountain in the way of your ministry? Begin to act in service, authenticity and authority to be strengthened in the very place of service. This is Jesus' conference of authority. As we serve His people, so we are stronger. As we walk out each moment in Him, we become more aware of His presence and promises. The royal authority comes to us as His power flows through us when we act in His will. We have the power in the name of Jesus as we take up our responsibilities. Start now. Today. Walk in His purpose so we may be strengthened in Him and have His heart, will and authority conferred upon us.

By your words I can see where I'm going;
they throw a beam of light on my dark path.
I've committed myself and I'll never turn back
from living by your righteous order.
Everything's falling apart on me, God;
put me together again with your Word.
Adorn me with your finest sayings, God;
teach me your holy rules.
My life is as close as my own hands,
but I don't forget what you have revealed.
The wicked do their best to throw me off
track, but I don't swerve an inch from your
course. I inherited your book on living; it's
mine forever– what a gift! And how happy
it makes me! I concentrate on doing exactly
what you say– I always have and always will.

Psalms 119: 105-112

Mine Forever!

A birthday is coming and the birthday girl has been asked what she wants. The truth is that I have all I need. I have Jesus! I have light, direction, purpose and purity of heart. I have a promised eternity, a happy family, a wonderful staff, and so much more. I am completely blessed. My life is far from perfect. I am walking through trials on every hand where it seems like everything around me is falling apart but God puts me together each morning with His word. He adorns me with His finest words and they drip like honey on my soul. I inherited this book of life and the instructions on living which I will not ever turn my back upon. It is a gift that makes me happy to concentrate on as I determine how to do exactly what He says-I always have and always will. His holy rules are as close as my own life and I do obey them because I love them. Living in His righteousness is my gift. As I approach the celebration of birthday years, I think of all the goodness, His love, and all the things He has brought me through. His love for me is the absolute best gift. Things will fade and pass but God's word hidden in our hearts is forever. "Summing it all up, friends, I'd say you'll do best by filling your minds and meditating on things true, noble, reputable, authentic, compelling, gracious—the best, not the worst; the beautiful, not the ugly; things to praise, not things to curse. Put into practice what you learned from me, what you heard and saw and realized. Do that, and God, who makes everything work together, will work you into his most excellent harmonies."

Philippians 4:8-9 MSG

It is His word that lights the dark path, gives light and guides through the tough times. Invest in Him for His word is mine forever! Gifts come and go but His word is forever!

That's exactly what Jesus did. He didn't make it easy for himself by avoiding people's troubles, but waded right in and helped out. "I took on the troubles of the troubled," is the way Scripture puts it. Even if it was written in Scripture long ago, you can be sure it's written for us. God wants the combination of his steady, constant calling and warm, personal counsel in Scripture to come to characterize us, keeping us alert for whatever he will do next. May our dependably steady and warmly personal God develop maturity in you so that you get along with each other as well as Jesus gets along with us all. Then we'll be a choir—not our voices only, but our very lives singing in harmony in a stunning anthem to the God and Father of our Master Jesus!

Romans 15: 3-6

Constant Calling!

God desires His warm, personal counsel and His steady, constant calling from His word to characterize our lives. He doesn't want us to be self-absorbed but rather mature and harmonious in our affection towards others. Situations can sometimes bring out the worst in us where we are not as we should be in our lives. He wants us to be alert for what He is doing. He wants us to be ready and eager to step out into His calling at any moment in life. Those moments can be something as simple as praying with a waitress, who one can tell is struggling with a problem, to intercession over a situation that only God can move into and change. I recently read a book written by an author who became a millionaire by using Biblical principles without realizing the truth behind them. My heart hurt for him as I read His words about energies and higher beings like he had no concept of who God is. He was using the principles and even the scriptures for monetary gain effectively but had no concept of who God is in our lives. How sad it is to me that so many approaches are based on the fullness of this life and they miss the truth of the constant calling. They hear it, feel it and misinterpret it to be an energy of Earth of some alien source outside them without grasping that God is softly and tenderly urging them towards a relationship with Him. There is so much falseness and manipulation in our world to the truth of God that many miss out on His quiet calling and fall into the traps of cultural beliefs and norms. The constant calling has a purpose of aligning us to Him and to each other in relationship like a choir singing a harmonious hymn. There is dissonance or disagreement in the notes sometimes as they are associated but not always in perfect agreement but they still go into the same song because their alignment is to Him. Align with God, hear His constant calling, become a part of His chorus.

As they led him off, they made Simon, a man from Cyrene who happened to be coming in from the countryside, carry the cross behind Jesus. A huge crowd of people followed, along with women weeping and carrying on. At one point Jesus turned to the women and said, "Daughters of Jerusalem, don't cry for me. Cry for yourselves and for your children. The time is coming when they'll say, 'Lucky the women who never conceived! Lucky the wombs that never gave birth! Lucky the breasts that never gave milk!' Then they'll start calling to the mountains, 'Fall down on us!' calling to the hills, 'Cover us up!' If people do these things to a live, green tree, can you imagine what they'll do with deadwood?"

Luke 23: 26-31

Coming Day!

My husband has been clearing tree debris for a month now since the last storm swept through here. It is surprising how much wood comes from one tree. One thing we have discussed is how much heavier and harder it is to dispose of a green tree versus a dead wood tree. As Jesus was walking to the cross, disfigured and beaten, the women who had followed Him and others began to lament. Their weeping and wailing was obviously getting on his nerves, so He turns back to them and reveals the truth of the end times we are approaching. He says not to weep for Him but to weep for ourselves because the day is coming where we will wish we had not had children and will beg for an end to the sorrow of life. If those who were "Godly" were willing to sacrifice God's son, what would they do in the name of religion throughout our lives? Look at Hitler and his attack on the Jewish people. Look at the wars of religion throughout history from Bloody Mary to the protestant cleansing. History teaches us that the truth is always surviving but continues to be attacked and smothered through "religion". Deadwood or Green tree? Are you alive in Him, allowing Him to flow through you no matter the circumstances or are you dead wood, just fodder waiting to be kindling in the fire? The Coming Days will be full of disruption, distress and folly. The future will look dim but God Himself knows you and if you are in The Vine, the Spirit flows through you. Be careful to stay rooted and full of His purpose so that when the smoke clears, you are still alive in His purpose. Deceptive forces are definitely aligning. The end is coming. Jesus is preparing to return to catch His bride away. Are you ready?

They were puzzled, wondering what to make of this. Then, out of nowhere it seemed, two men, light cascading over them, stood there. The women were awestruck and bowed down in worship. The men said, "Why are you looking for the Living One in a cemetery? He is not here, but raised up. Remember how he told you when you were still back in Galilee that he had to be handed over to sinners, be killed on a cross, and in three days rise up?" Then they remembered Jesus' words.

Luke 24: 4-8

Words Remembered!

Memory is a funny and interesting thing! We remember things that are unimportant and forget things we should remember. Age affects memory, as does nutrition, stress, hydration and lifestyle. As a brain trainer, I see lots of folks who struggle with memory and for various reasons. One of the hardest diagnoses is Alzheimer's or dementia...because one loses those things held in memory. Working on memory exercises to build memory's skill is an arduous task but strengthening those neural connections is critical. The other day as my family sat around a table, we recalled an event we all remembered but it was interesting how we remembered it so differently. Each of us had a different piece of it, then my mom, who has incredible memory added a detail and it was like a lightbulb because suddenly our individual pieces all made sense. In this passage of scripture, we see these women who have traveled, loved and worshiped Jesus, arrive at the tomb full of grief and traumatized by His crucifixion. They see the tomb opened and they are puzzled as they are confronted by two men suddenly appearing in a cascade of light. They realize these are angels and bow to worship. These angels then remind the women of the words Jesus had spoken. Then the verse says, "Then they remembered Jesus' words." It took a reminder to trigger that memory because they were in grief. Emotions can make our memory recall very hard. In fact, many people suppress both good and bad memories as a safety feature to their psyche. These ladies were so much in love and grief that the words of the Living One were hidden in their minds behind the reality of what they had experienced. But they were recorded there. And when they were reminded, they remembered. Scripture tells us to hide His words in our heart so we don't sin against Him but we also need to hide them in our hearts so we can refresh our memory when the emotions of life overwhelm us. We are created in His image. He has called us by name. We are His. He will never leave us nor forsake us. These are just a few reminders to encase as we go through our days so that in times of stress and emotional upheaval, we can remember His words of life. Remember the Living One is not among the dead of this Earth. He is alive forevermore and at the right hand of God making intercession for us. Remember His words.

Jesus answered by quoting Deuteronomy: "It takes more than bread to stay alive. It takes a steady stream of words from God's mouth."

Matthew 4:4

Steady Stream!

Overwhelmed! Taking it all in at once can drown you whether that be water, information, criticism or beauty. There is an old saying that says "too much of a good thing is a bad thing". This is talking about excess or indulgence. We all know that chocolate is delicious but too much will tear your stomach up and make you gain weight because it is full of sugar and magnesium which controls the bowel. Too much water can make you sick but it is a necessity in life. Too much is too much. This verse struck me this morning as I faced a situation in my life of too much. I had overdone and was having trouble walking. Then I remembered who my Great Physician was and came into His presence. He dropped this nugget of truth on me. It takes more than the delights and nutrients of this world to live. It takes a steadiness of His word to right our lives and put us on an even balance. We often get shifted off balance in our lives from our overdoing in our work/life balance. We choose too much of one thing or another and the imbalance throws us off. Our center of gravity is in Him. When we try to shift our center onto other things then the careening starts which is a warning sign of harmful things to come. That still small voice shouldn't have to shout inside our heads. We must learn to hear it. Jesus was tired and exhausted. He was tormented day and night by Satan for forty days. He was hungry and we all know the "hangry" that comes from hunger. He was in a desert place, thirsting and I am sure He felt very alone but He turned to the steady stream when all else failed him. He turned to The Word, the life course, the source, the Living Water that He was, turned to The Word. Get this please. God Himself in the flesh turned to the wordsmith of knowledge recorded in the scriptures to sustain Him! This is because His word is life. It is alive. It is a steady stream in our desert place. It is our sustainable resource that never runs dry. His words live and breathe in our being. They are LIFE! We cannot quench a thirst without the life-source. No one, can stop the power of the Word. It is infinite. In the beginning was The Word and the Word was with God and the Word was God and the Word came to dwell among men. We have The Word. It is the steady stream. It is our choice to drink.

But don't let it faze you. Stick with what you learned and believed, sure of the integrity of your teachers—why, you took in the sacred Scriptures with your mother's milk! There's nothing like the written Word of God for showing you the way to salvation through faith in Christ Jesus. Every part of Scripture is God-breathed and useful one way or another—showing us truth, exposing our rebellion, correcting our mistakes, training us to live God's way. Through the Word we are put together and shaped up for the tasks God has for us.

2 Timothy 3:14-17

God Breathed!

As I went through training, updating, learning and refreshing of my skills the last few days, I realized that we are God purposed moment to moment. The Word that is in us and has been trained in us is God-breathed in the very essence. As I sat with different people and embraced differentiation in their perspectives and perceptions of the same concepts I was fascinated not only by the Word but by the impact. There is a song called "Somewhere Out There" which talks about how connected we are to the same moonlight that we look at even when we feel disconnected. It is written as a lonely song of connection for those missing one another to reconnect. We all look at the same moon and yet our perspective of it differs. This God breathed and God placed ball of matter that reflects the light from a star is inspiration to many of us because it seems so mysterious. Grasping the intimacy of our own God being so intimate to us that He breathed into us at conception to give us life in our mother's womb. The spark of life, the mystery cannot be drilled down to science no matter how hard we try to replicate it because it is God-breathed. No AI, computer nor technology can replicate the intimacy of God's breath. It fascinates me that we can attempt to replicate and imitate so much of life and things in it but the very essence of each of us is unique and impossible to replicate. We are God-breathed. His Word alive in us is God-Breathed. The very essence of who He is dwells in us-uniquely and indispensably. There is not another You! People can try to duplicate what you do, replicate your voice, your mannerisms and even your actions but it cannot be done. As I sat at a table of other wonderful women learning and sharing, one of them voiced this incredible concept in an admirable way and I thought, wow, she is so wise and impressive...I would love to have her wisdom. Then in the next moment, she voiced a similarly positive thought towards me. It dawned on me at that moment that God's infinity is breathed into our beings creating a unique and wonderful person with the sole purpose of recognizing Him. In our rejoicing of Him, He accelerates our ability to become more like Him. God breathers...God sharers...God inhabitants. We are His. We carry Him in us. His Word breathes life into us and through us. What a powerful blessing this is!

"When you come looking for me, you'll find me. "Yes, when you get serious about finding me and want it more than anything else, I'll make sure you won't be disappointed." God's Decree. "I'll turn things around for you. I'll bring you back from all the countries into which I drove you"– God's Decree–"bring you home to the place from which I sent you off into exile. You can count on it.

Jeremiah 29:13-14

Serious Searching!

Why is it that we find what we are looking for in the last place we think to look? Because we quit searching once we find it! In Jeremiah, God is speaking to the Israelites about His plans for them. We often quote His promises about knowing the plans He has for us from Jeremiah 29:11 but we leave out the finding out the plan from Him which is stated in 13. In other words, we find the promise but fail to look at retrieval of that promise. I read a story recently of an archaeologist who spent her lifetime looking for something she had already found. As a young lady, she was in the desert on a dig which unearthed a wonderful discovery but she failed to bring the necessary tools to retrieve the precious find so she marked the area then left to go retrieve her tools. In doing so, she left behind the treasure. A sandstorm came which delayed her and although she had modern technology which had marked her original find location, she searched for years and sifted sand for years looking but never saw the treasure again. Lots of people have commented over the years about her quests, from naysayers who doubt the original find to people telling her to just move on but she is still searching for that treasure because she wants it more than anything else. God tells us that when we come looking for Him and His plans with a single minded devotion, serious searching, then we will find Him and not be disappointed. A lot of people passively approach God. They read a devotional or good book, they pray before dinner, they say goodnight prayers and try to be good, they ask for God's guidance and blessings but they never seek Him for themselves with all their hearts. If we spend time on all the other things of life, flitting here and there, work, home, vacation and just continuously living without His heart, we miss out on the true purpose of life. The only purpose of life is in Him. The only true fulfillment to withstand it all is in Him. When we truly seek Him with diligence and get serious about searching for His heart, we find the treasure that can never be lost. Let me tell you a secret. There is no self help book better than this one scripture. God's word is alive and He says, when you get serious about finding me and want it MORE than anything else you dream about or desire, you'll find me and I'll make sure you won't be disappointed! I will turn things around for you and bring you back from all the places you have been driven...home from exile. My favorite part-You can count on it. Obviously you didn't hear that or you'd be shouting in excitement. The treasure is found! The goal is reached! The game is won! The dream is realized! The healing is here! The serious search leads to the ultimate arrival. You can quit seeking anything else when you realize that He is the answer! You can count on Him! Question: what are you seeking that is more important than the God of the Universe who has promised you won't be disappointed in what He does for you if you will seek Him with all your heart? Read this verse again. Seek and you shall find Him. His heart is for you! Seek Him!

This is my life work: helping people understand and respond to this Message. It came as a sheer gift to me, a real surprise, God handling all the details. When it came to presenting the Message to people who had no background in God's way, I was the least qualified of any of the available Christians. God saw to it that I was equipped, but you can be sure that it had nothing to do with my natural abilities.

And so here I am, preaching and writing about things that are way over my head, the inexhaustible riches and generosity of Christ. My task is to bring out in the open and make plain what God, who created all this in the first place, has been doing in secret and behind the scenes all along. Through followers of Jesus like yourselves gathered in churches, this extraordinary plan of God is becoming known and talked about even among the angels!

Ephesians 3:7-10

Real Surprise!

Today is a celebration of life not because it is a birthday but rather because another day of purposeful life has been graced to me. Like Paul in this chapter of Ephesians, life is a sheer gift to me. Each day is a real surprise and blessing because I know I am the least among people qualified to share His word and yet He has given me this opportunity. God sees to it each day that I am equipped to do what He calls me to do not through my natural abilities but through His extraordinary plan. His ways are not my ways. His purpose is different from mine. His assurance is not through my ability but through my willingness. God gives us each a plan and purpose unique to us so we may do according to what He asks. Our life work is to help people understand and respond to His Message of Life. This is our gift we open daily when we open our eyes from sleep. The real surprise is not what Christ has done but rather that He chose us to parlay His inexhaustible riches and generosity to others. He has called us to bring out into the open and make plain what God has done through Christ Jesus. This secret, behind the scenes God has called us and purposed us for this time, this place, this day, this moment to share His generosity and His goodness and His faithfulness and His love and His joy and His wealth of knowledge, His fruit, His table, His plan, His purpose to all in our frame of reference. We are famous and talked about among the angels because we carry His light! We carry His secret into the open! We carry Him. We carry His heart, His love and His way, truth and life. We are the real surprise. What gift will I open in His presence today? Love to the broken, joy to the hurting, comfort to the grieving, laughter to the lonely? The lovely surprise is that He chose me to carry Him. He chose me just like He chose each person He tasks. Our purposes and our marketplace of ministry may look very different but He has called us and purposed us with yet unopened gifts to be used for His glory. What will you open in His presence today?

"I can't stand your religious meetings.
I'm fed up with your conferences
and conventions.
I want nothing to do with
your religion projects,
your pretentious slogans and goals.
I'm sick of your fund-raising schemes,
your public relations and image making.
I've had all I can take of your
noisy ego-music.
When was the last time you sang to me?
Do you know what I want?
I want justice—oceans of it.
I want fairness—rivers of it.
That's what I want. That's all I want.

Amos 5:21-24

Image Making!

As I pen this 12th devotional in my 12th collection of devotionals, my mind thinks and processes all the wonderful tidbits I have gleaned. I think of the years and time wasted in other pursuits and I glory in the knowledge that God saw fit to continue to work in me through it all. In this portion of Amos, God is fed up with all the noise and clutter that has become the standard of that day. I can only imagine His thoughts of our current status. He spoke through Amos to the people admonishing them that He was tired of the play at religious things with no sincerity of heart. He wants justice and fairness. My first devotional book was titled "Oceans of God's Love" because that is what He gives us. He gives us unexpected and unending waves of love but demands oceans of justice in return. As He is the judge, the judgment days are coming where those who rejected His oceans of love will meet the oceans of justice He nets out with the rivers of fairness. We don't see a lot of fairness in this life now but we will see His justice. He bides His time, patiently calling to give us the opportunity to get out of our image making schemes into the truth of His love. The news reported another shark attack. The person who went into the waters knew the reality of sharks in that particular area but chose to go in so they could make an image of themselves surfing the wave. They lost their life to poor judgment on their part. It is a tragedy we see too often repeating. Our poor judgment skewed by the image making world draws us into the judgment of self. We invite the world into a place where God only should dwell and when justice is meted out, we fall apart wondering why. We are so consumed by our "Barbie world" that we have constantly construed a falsehood of imagery that we play at rather than walking in truth and light. This may seem harsh but the judgment day is coming where justice will be met. God is calling us to His image rather than the image making of self. He has called us away from the "I" into the "Him" but we are consumed with the "I" so much that we would rather hold the iPhone and take the selfie than to sacrifice the time it takes to humble ourselves in prayer. The consequence of image making is a violation of the commandment to love God alone first as we indulge in our selfish ways. The business next door to mine is called Selfieisms. It is a place people go to project a lie. It is a place to go to build up self. I am not against this small business as they are simply capturing the demand of our culture. I am sad that the church has become this. We are so deceived now that photo booths are more prevalent in churches than miracles. We have taken a place of dedication to God and turned it into a shrine of selfish parties and pretentious slogans. Church has become big business rather than a place of sacrifice and outreach. We are consumed with songs about me and I rather than Him and Holiness. God is calling. The waters of life are responding to His call for fairness and judgment. The day of reckoning is at hand. It is time to put aside the campaigns of selfish ambition and once again turn our eyes to Him. The sharks of life are in the waters devouring the souls of men. The call for judgment has been issued. Will we turn again to His oceans of love or will we be consumed by our image making selves? The choice is ours. He calls us in waves of love to abandon the pursuit of self and once again turn to our first love.

"To you who are ready for the truth, I say this: Love your enemies. Let them bring out the best in you, not the worst. When someone gives you a hard time, respond with the supple moves of prayer for that person. If someone slaps you in the face, stand there and take it. If someone grabs your shirt, giftwrap your best coat and make a present of it. If someone takes unfair advantage of you, use the occasion to practice the servant life. No more payback. Live generously.

Luke 6:27-30

Supple Moves!

Moving easily with plenty of flexibility feels like a thing of the past for my body but not for my spirit. In fact, just like the body, the more you flex the spirit, the more it learns to move easily. In Luke, the doctor advises us to be ready for the truth, then follows with, love your enemies and allow them to bring out the best in you and not the worst. This is very hard in the dog eat dog world we live in because it is exactly the opposite of what we are taught. We are told to stand up for ourselves, don't let people walk over us and to speak our minds. However all of these are contradictory to scripture and the Word of God. The Word tells us to be submissive to Him and allow Him to fight our battles. As we played Monopoly with the family, we quickly found that the underdog became the top dog when he quietly purchased the railroads, then another set of property, then persisted making deals without giving up. It was frustrating to be the one working so hard but not winning and so it is in life. When we feel like we work hard to achieve our dreams but they stay just out of our grasp or we constantly work hard without the reward we feel we deserve, we feel defeated. When the work to achieve becomes overwhelming, we lose sight of the true goal and begin to focus on the here/now which leads us into places of frustration instead of freedom. Supple moves come from much practice. Flexibility comes from being stretched often and consistently in our spiritual lives. When the trials and storms make us stretched to our breaking point but we lean a little further into Him, we build the flexibility to become supple movers in His word. We learn to respond instantly and completely to His call. We learn to rest and lean on Him rather than our own ability. My body needs stretching to become more flexible and efficient. When I sit around too much, I get tight and my muscles become stagnant and unyielding. This same thing happens when we fail to exercise our spirit. We become stuck and staid, legalistic and judgmental. But when we learn His moves and His harmony, we begin to move gracefully in the dance with the King. We begin to see and feel the harmonies of His music and mysteries. We begin to understand the ways of His working and why He instructs us to live generously. When we practice His love, we become ready for the supple moves of truth. We begin to allow the negative to bring out the sweet tones and harmonies in our lives. We become more than a simple tune but rather a symphony of praise. We respond instantly and completely in love and joy to His presence in others. The key is to exercise it. Embrace the challenges and hard times as the wonderful harmonies of His love rather than negativity. It will change your perspective and make you more flexible.

In light of all this, here's what I want you to do. While I'm locked up here, a prisoner for the Master, I want you to get out there and walk—better yet, run!—on the road God called you to travel. I don't want any of you sitting around on your hands. I don't want anyone strolling off, down some path that goes no-where. And mark that you do this with humility and discipline—not in fits and starts, but steadily, pouring yourselves out for each other in acts of love, alert at noticing differences and quick at mending fences.

Ephesians 4:1-3

Fits & Starts!

Today has been a morning of fits and starts! When I finally sat back down to do my devotional, I was in a rush and was feeling like I was in a marathon as I read this passage. Our lives are filled with the unexpected and unknown, yet we do not have to be led on a circus parade of acts and performances if we remember who He is. As Paul sat in prison, he sent a letter to the church to not become a place of fits and starts but to be purposeful in the journey towards God. No wandering off on bunny trails of crusades and running from place to place to experience God but a purposeful path that follows the pattern of His leading. When we get caught up in the next thing or the next place or the next happenings in our world, we get off track and instead of a steady growth we become a yo-yo diet with our spiritual health.

Instead we are to steadily pour into one another in acts of love, alert at noticing when things are not as they should be and mending fences that have gotten broken by carelessness. God called us to travel this road with one another in love and humility but also with discipline in our lives. We are called to be all we should be in this way. We should honor one another, take time for one another and think to bless one another as we travel. We are not on a road to get ahead of each other as our destination remains the same. We are called to run along with each other supporting each other in the race of life. That means stopping to take time to lift one another up in all things. I am as guilty as any of getting so busy that I fail to check in with others as I should and this recently broke my heart as I had a sweet friend who truly needed me in a time of pain and sorrow but she didn't come to me because of my busyness. I have mended that fence now and am trying to take more care but when the days seem to overwhelm and overload, I am careful now to remember that others feel alone too! I am grateful for those who reach out to care for me and I am aiming to be better at doing the same. So as I sit to deliberately take time today, I am grateful to have the opportunity to speak into the lives of others and know that they too will stop to carry me in times of need. Who are you carrying or stopping to help along in this busy journey of life? Are you steadily walking and running or are you getting distracted by other things that do not truly matter to the final destination? Examine and reflect. Mend the fences, repair the relationships and get focused on the purposeful life.

They came to the edge of the village where they were headed. He acted as if he were going on but they pressed him: "Stay and have supper with us. It's nearly evening; the day is done." So he went in with them. And here is what happened: He sat down at the table with them. Taking the bread, he blessed and broke and gave it to them. At that moment, open-eyed, wide-eyed, they recognized him. And then he disappeared.

Luke 24: 28-31

Recognizing Him!

This passage has always fascinated me because I have a hard time picturing why these people who walked and talked with Jesus every day didn't recognize Him as they spent hours walking and talking with Him. They only recognized Him when He prayed with authority. In this world of chaos, AI and digital mockups, it is easy to mistake people for one another. I have two students that I train with and their moms look similar, such that when I took one student out, I just glanced towards the mom, made an assumption it was the parent I needed to speak with and began talking about her daughter until the little girl laughed! She realized what I had done and said, that's not my mom. We laughed about it and then the next week, I actually did it again! Yesterday as they both sat in my lobby, I started to take a "twins" picture because they are so similar to me. Both moms know each other and now it is a huge laughing joke each time I train the kids back to back. In my haste, I made a mistake because I did not fully look. That is the reason these people didn't recognize Jesus. They were consumed with their own agenda and He was dead in their minds so their minds did not conceive the possibility. We do this all the time. We fail to recognize Him in our lives in our daily tasks because we are consumed with our day to day so that we fail to accept the possibility of Him living and breathing in us and through us in the minute by minute. We get so caught up in the next thing that we fail to recognize His hand in us actively moving until the powerful authority brings about a miracle or recognition in us. As we walk along in life with others, who are they seeing? Are they seeing Jesus in us or are we so busy with self that He is shoved aside unseen? What do our mannerisms and actions tell others about who He is in us?

We humans keep brainstorming options and plans,
but God's purpose prevails.

Proverbs 19:21

Prevailing Purpose!

Kept hearing a dog bark fiercely last evening and went to bed frustrated about it as it made it hard to sleep. Then I woke up in the middle of the night, just a few hours later, in a complete panic as I realized that my small dog wasn't in the house. This is bad as we have coyotes out here. I called and called but no response, so I woke my husband and asked him to help me. We remembered that just before bed, he had gone to close the garage and sure enough, our small dog had gotten trapped in the garage because he had snuck out of the house. He was very thirsty and grateful to be back in once he was saved, because it had been hard on him. Just like us, his plan to go out and do his thing backfired on him. So many times we humans brainstorm options and plans but we do not have the right answers so our plans fail. We do not know it all. God's purpose and plans prevail no matter what and when we align in His way, we will not fail. Oftentimes, we get so caught up in our plans that we miss the purpose of God in our lives. "Take good counsel and accept correction– that's the way to live wisely and well." Proverbs 19:20 MSG. This is the verse that precedes the verse for today. Good counsel, Godly counsel and accountability to it as well as acceptance of correction and constructive criticism leads us in the path of knowledge. Instead of trying to do it all ourselves, we learn, grow and change through God's plan. Instead of running into our own ways and getting stuck in the traps of our own making, if we will trust God and receive wise counsel rather than stop trying to just brainstorm our way out with our options and plans, our lives will run much easier. As I think about that puppy wanting his own way, realizing he was trapped, then hollering out over and over....I think we are often just like this....just stop! We need to yield to His purpose and plan. That is the way of peace and wise counsel.

If you've gotten anything at all out of following Christ, if his love has made any difference in your life, if being in a community of the Spirit means anything to you, if you have a heart, if you care— then do me a favor: Agree with each other, love each other, be deep-spirited friends. Don't push your way to the front; don't sweet-talk your way to the top. Put yourself aside, and help others get ahead. Don't be obsessed with getting your own advantage. Forget yourselves long enough to lend a helping hand.

Philippians 2: 1-4

Deep Spirited!

There is a story about a mouse that had fallen into a bucket of cream when he tried to take a drink. He was drowning until suddenly others joined him and they began to swim quickly encouraging each other as it got harder and harder until the cream was now butter which they could rest upon and enjoy to their hearts' content. Imagine the delight of a person finding their cream had been churned into butter without them lifting a finger, well, unless they saw the mice! Deep-spirited means being in togetherness through the tough times and not being an all about me person. It is a genuinely humble spirit that isn't obsessed with their own advantages but willing to put themselves to the side for others. My mom is one of these truly deep spirited people and everyone knows it. I will confess that sometimes I get frustrated with it because she prioritizes people's needs so far above her own that she risks her own health often. Her heart is so big and generous that her own life fails to matter when someone else is in trouble or needs something which is why everyone loves her completely and wholly. She is an example of what true agape love is...sacrifices for the whole. His example to us was just this: He will provide all our needs if we will but trust and do for others sacrificially. The mouse would've drowned and the others missed out on the blessing of the butter if they had not been willing to sacrifice their own comfort for another. We are not called to be less but to be more. The path to becoming more in power, authority, wealth, health and eternity is in the willingness to be less. Christ Himself gave all including His own life in order to redeem us. God put forth the plan and was waiting for man. Man failed God but God in His deep love for His creation, gave His Son as an atonement for the law to redeem that old covenant into newness through His perfect sacrifice. Today I challenge you to give of yourselves sacrificially. Give your meal money or your meal away today and pray for the person receiving. Give something you love or cherish of great value to another In sacrifice to demonstrate His love. Let Him lead you into the path of giving up that which is holding you from being all He desires you to be. God wants us to be happy, healthy, wise and even wealthy in Him. He does not desire us to be self indulgent and over extend ourselves. He wants us to become like Him: Full of sacrificial love and devotion.

But if God himself has taken up residence in your life, you can hardly be thinking more of yourself than of him. Anyone, of course, who has not welcomed this invisible but clearly present God, the Spirit of Christ, won't know what we're talking about. But for you who welcome him, in whom he dwells—even though you still experience all the limitations of sin—you yourself experience life on God's terms. It stands to reason, doesn't it, that if the alive-and-present God who raised Jesus from the dead moves into your life, he'll do the same thing in you that he did in Jesus, bringing you alive to himself? When God lives and breathes in you (and he does, as surely as he did in Jesus), you are delivered from that dead life. With his Spirit living in you, your body will be as alive as Christ's!

Roman 8:9-11

God's Terms!

Terms we agree on form an agreement. These can be contracts or other formalities but the terms matter for they are the basis of the agreement. God's terms of residence in our lives are defined. The first and foremost is that He has priority. We cannot think more of ourselves than of Him. As a commandment, it says that we should love no other above Him. As a reminder, it is stated that we Love the Lord our God with all our heart, soul, mind and strength. Life on God's terms means living in Him as He dwells in us. The terms of acceptance of His son as a sacrifice for our sins means we choose to put God above all else and He does the same for us. If we begin to truly walk in the terms of the covenant that God made with us, we will walk in true life. Freedom isn't free unless we walk in it. The Spirit of God that raised Christ from the dead dwells in us when we accept the terms of agreement. Our freedom of life isn't about lifestyle but it is about our mindset. If we walk in bondage in our mind, then we are not fully accepting the terms God granted us. Accepting God's terms means accepting that He gave all for us so that we might give freely of ourselves to Him. We are created for Him, by Him, through Him and yet He still gave us the best terms. I remember the negotiations when we bought our house. We asked for certain things and the sellers agreed with some and rejected others until we finally found an agreement of terms. I will say that some of these terms were not what I wanted but in order to have the freedom to dwell in this house, and to call it my own, I had to accept the terms. Freedom in Salvation came with a price tag that Jesus paid but in order for us to walk in this freedom, we must be willing to agree to the terms. This Salvation is for all who choose to believe and accept that Jesus is God's son who came to dwell among us in order to save us by His superior sacrifice. The atonement came and the resurrection brought new life. We can walk in that freedom of new life by accepting the terms that God reigns over all in our lives. Thus ever present and God is alive, living and breathing in us when we accept the terms to be delivered from the death sentence of sin. Our body is alive in Him. We are His dwelling place. We may have the limitations of flesh for now as we abide on Earth but our spirit lives, moves and has being in Him. We do not have to walk around beat up and pressed down but rather we walk in life and freedom because He has already won! Our circumstances may look bleak but that is an earthly mindset. Our living mindset under God's terms says Greater is He that is in me than he that is in this world. We gotta quit walking under men's terms and begin to see the salvation of God. His terms are life, freedom and peace. His terms are health, wealth and beauty. His terms are above all kingdoms, powers and forces of nature. Today is the day to begin to declare the victory of His terms and walk in Him. Quit living in the old man's rubble listening to satan's lies and move into the castle He created for you with freedom and provision. The same God who raised Jesus from the dead dwells in us. These are His terms. Now walk in them!

How wonderful, how beautiful,
when brothers and sisters get along!
It's like costly anointing oil
flowing down head and beard,
Flowing down Aaron's beard,
flowing down the collar of his
priestly robes.
It's like the dew on Mount Hermon
flowing down the slopes of Zion.
Yes, that's where God commands
the blessing,
ordains eternal life.

Psalms 133: 1-3

Flowing Down!

I do not know anyone who would not desire God's blessings to cover their lives. In Psalms, David reveals where God commands blessing and ordains eternal life. It is in communion and getting along. There is nothing so abhorrent to God as seeing His children fuss and squabble. How do I know this? Because I am a mother and this is the one thing that drives me nuts. Our world/society is fraught with the competition and one upness of being top dog. The highly competitive vein means that we are constantly pitted against one another instead of working together to build. Anointing flows when we are in agreement and unity. God dwells in the place of unity and performs miracles in this. When we are contending with one another, He will not bless that place until we are in harmony with Him. This does not mean we have to agree on all things but it does mean we must set our eyes and heart on Him. What would our world look like if we were pulling together and helping one another? I know from experience how powerful that is. I watched our country come together after 9/11 and the harmony was incredible until the head of contention and politics reared again. It is sad that it takes tragedy and horror to get our attention. I was surprised at the Covid19 response and how contentious it all was until I realized that we were pitted against one another rather than in unity. It matters. Unity matters. God is calling His people to a place of agreement in Him. He says where two or three are gathered in His name, He will be there and do mighty things that they ask. I am challenging each of us to draw closer to Him. Pray with your brothers and sisters in Christ. Quit being against them in word/deed. This negative sentiment or putting down, harms the peace and disrupts what God is doing. If you want blessings in your life, be a blessing by walking in harmony rather than contending with your brethren and your sisters in Christ. Blessings may come through hard times but God uses us to be the hands extended. Reach out. Unite. Pray, Feed in word and deed. Allow His Holy Anointing of Blessings into your life through harmony. Get along with your brothers and sisters in Christ. Stop it! Just stop the drama and the back talk. Stop the rebellion and the being in control. Get along! Reach out today and tell your brothers and sisters how much you care. Be the difference.

Summing it all up, friends, I'd say you'll do best by filling your minds and meditating on things true, noble, reputable, authentic, compelling, gracious—the best, not the worst; the beautiful, not the ugly; things to praise, not things to curse. Put into practice what you learned from me, what you heard and saw and realized. Do that, and God, who makes everything work together, will work you into his most excellent harmonies.

Philippians 4:8-9

The Focus!

When the lens on my phone finally focused on the thing I was trying to take a picture of, the moment had passed. I had lost the innate detail I wanted because the lens wouldn't focus. It kept filling with all the other things around it and dancing from object to object that was brightly colored like the lens had ADD. In Phillippians, Paul talks to us through them, telling us to sum it all up. Summing it all up means to add it up, stack it, pull it together into one lump sum. He says sum it up best by filling our minds and meditating on what is true, noble, reputable, authentic, compelling, gracious-the best not the worst, the beautiful not the ugly; things to praise not things to curse. He says sum it up then put it into practice and when we do this, God who makes everything work together for good to please Him will work us into the sum total of that beauty. Did you know that white is the presence of all colors? If one color is missing, the light isn't white. If the summing isn't done with all the pieces, then the end total won't be as God intended. He designed you to be a part of the light. You are light that He created and lit for a purpose and He has perfect plans for you. You are an intricate part of the sum total of this life so it is best to fill your mind with the good things, the perfect things, the things that are described in this word. If we focus our lens of life on "whatever things are true, whatever things are noble, whatever things are just, whatever things are pure, whatever things are lovely, whatever things are of good report," and we do as instructed which is "if there is any virtue and if there is anything praiseworthy—meditate on these things.", then our lives will be focused on the sum total of who He is instead of who we are and what we are going through. If we focus on these things and meditate on them constantly, then we reach the sum total of who HE is-the pure light, pure love, perfect God. So, what are you focusing on? Readjust your lens today. If it isn't pure, true, lovely and a part of the sum total of Him, let it go!

Keep your focus. Sum it up to the good. God is working excellent harmony in your life. No matter what today looks like-allow it to breathe Him. 35 years ago today, I lost my brother and I still don't understand why but I have and will continue to allow it to work in perfect harmony despite my grief. Nothing is too hard that it cannot be solved by God. Just rest in that and keep focused.

Dear friends, do you think you'll get anywhere in this if you learn all the right words but never do anything? Does merely talking about faith indicate that a person really has it? For instance, you come upon an old friend dressed in rags and half-starved and say, "Good morning, friend! Be clothed in Christ! Be filled with the Holy Spirit!" and walk off without providing so much as a coat or a cup of soup—where does that get you? Isn't it obvious that God-talk without God-acts is outrageous nonsense?

James 2:14-17

God Conviction!

Confession time! I am guilty of a lot of God talk and a wobble in my faith walk! Faith requires action. I am an action kinda girl but the God-acts without the bungee cord are a little tough on this girl. I like bungee jumping because the cord is my security. I like skydiving and taking a leap, if I can see where I am landing. Fear happens in the pause or waiting place. Fear happens when you are waiting on the enough but it sure is too close for comfort. Fear strikes when the impossible meets God's possible but it isn't revealed yet. Talking about faith is one thing but walking in it is another. I know God heals and He has healed me many times but I also know when my back is hurting badly, it is harder to walk in faith, believing. However, this is the doing part of faith. The doing part is the God conviction part. The knowing He is and He has rather than He could if He would. The knowing is, the God conviction. The God acts are, the stepping out in faith towards what seems impossible all the while knowing it is possible. Whether it is your bank account, your body, your emotional load or something else, He is still the God of the impossible. He is. We cannot speak the words and fail to act. This is not a magic show with Jesus as the magician. Saying "I trust you Lord" requires stepping out in faith believing that He will be enough. God is bigger than any problem, fear, need or even mountains we cannot move. He is able and He is willing and He will.

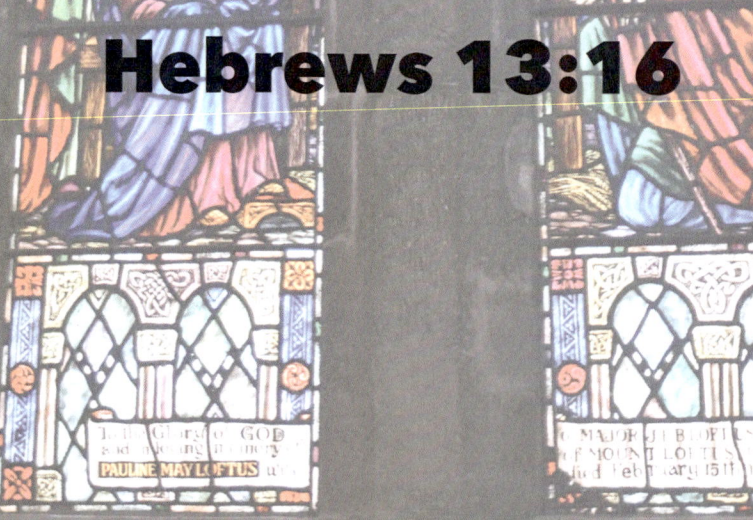

Make sure you don't take things for granted and go slack in working for the common good; share what you have with others. God takes particular pleasure in acts of worship–a different kind of "sacrifice"–that take place in kitchen and workplace and on the streets.

Hebrews 13:16

46

Particular Pleasure!

Did you know that God takes pleasure in you sweeping your floors and doing your everyday tasks? You see, He takes particular pleasure in us and in our acts of worship which can be our every day business that is done for common good. Sometimes we get so caught up in trying to do something miraculous that we forget the small things of everyday life that give God particular pleasure just by being in His presence. The day to day can become a drudge or a gift depending on how we approach it. If my getting up, dressed and ready to begin my day is focused on who He is instead of who I am, then I can start my day in confidence rather than dread. My day can be a day of blessing rather than a day of frustration. My day can be an uplifting moment rather than a day of boring tasks. My simple everyday tasks like washing dishes can become a gift of praise to God just by my mindset. Instead of looking ahead at my day with dread, I can look forward in delight to see what God is doing. What things are ahead for you today? Look at each moment as an opportunity that God has given you and sing through the frustrations into the glory. Share with others. Look ahead to possibilities. Embrace the sacrifice as unto God. Do not get weighed down by the lack but instead begin to focus on the, Who He is. Don't take your every day for granted because there are plenty of people who wish they could do the things you dread doing. Do whatever your hand finds to do with a grateful heart and count your blessings. Your day will change when you begin to see it as a day of possibilities rather than dreaded tasks. Mindset matters. Turn on the God perspective and experience His particular pleasure in you today. What can I do today to be His hand extended to others? Maybe it is just picking up trash off a parking lot and saying thank you God that I can bend over to pick up this piece of trash. Whatever it is, do it as unto Him with blessings on your lips rather than gripes! That is how to experience God's particular pleasure in us!

Are you hurting? Pray. Do you feel great? Sing. Are you sick? Call the church leaders together to pray and anoint you with oil in the name of the Master. Believing-prayer will heal you, and Jesus will put you on your feet. And if you've sinned, you'll be forgiven—healed inside and out.

James 5:13-15

Healed Inside!

Hurt happens to all of us. Sometimes the hurt is intentional but rarely. Most of the time, hurt happens because of carelessness in comments or actions of others. Often hurt happens because of our own choices. It is easy to talk about what one should do and harder to do it when it happens to you. I recently sat down with a sweet friend who lost her spouse not terribly long ago. As I saw the tears in her eyes from the loneliness and wondering of what was next, my heart engaged to remind me that we are all on a path or journey that includes pain, sorrow and loss but that same path also includes hope, dreams and futures. Sometimes our eyes are looking at the desert ground and the sandy soil so much that we miss the beautiful rainbows and the silver linings. One of my favorite songs is Blessings by Laura Story which asks:

"What if your blessings come through raindrops?
What if Your healing comes through tears?
And what if the thousand sleepless nights
are what it takes to know You're near?
And what if trials of this life are Your mercies in disguise?"

Our lives are not promised to be without trial and sorrow. That is the way of this Earth. What we are promised is that He will be with us through it all. I can honestly say that this year has been the hardest year in my memory in many ways but I have had harder in other ways. If I focus on counting my blessings and looking towards my future, my possibilities instead of looking at the ground I am currently in, my mindset will be much better. In this verse in James, we are instructed on how to pray in our surroundings and situations. It says if you are hurting, pray. If you are doing great, sing. If you are sick,, call the church and ask for the leaders to come anoint you and pray believing for you in Jesus' name. Then it clearly states that Believing prayer will heal you and put you on your feet. If you have sinned, you'll be forgiven, healed inside and out. It fascinates me that often Jesus healed in His ministry just like this. He would say, your sins are forgiven rather than you are healed. It frustrated those around Him who asked him about it, questioning His authority to do so. He responded by asking which was easier: the healing of the body or the forgiveness of sin. This got me pondering on why we so easily and readily accept His forgiveness without question now but are not so ready to accept the healing. We have no evidence of His forgiveness yet are ready to easily accept it. We have evidence of the pain and hurt so we hold onto that rather than accepting that it is in His control. It is our mindset. His word clearly states that by His stripes we are healed. Why then are we so eager to accept His death as atonement for our sin and His resurrection as proof of eternal life but we are not so open to accepting His stripes for our healing? I am as guilty of this as any other. The evidence of the pain overwrites the belief in the healing process. So today, I am praying for complete and utter confidence in the healing process inside. This means to be whole in my faith so my body can be healed. Do I believe that lack of faith causes lack of healing? In some instances. I believe God can and will, but I also know that it requires us to walk in the faith of His healing power. There are some He doesn't heal in our Earthly presence who have had faith and I don't always understand it. But I believe in miracles and I want to work on my inner healing so my faith can be a growing part of my inner being which leads to my outer healing. Lord, I believe but help my unbelief.

Everything was created through him; nothing–not one thing!–came into being without him. What came into existence was Life, and the Life was Light to live by. The Life-Light blazed out of the darkness; the darkness couldn't put it out.

John 1:3-5

Life-Light!

The dawn chases away the dark. Oh, I do understand the science that the Earth is rotating on its axis and revolving around the sun which is why we have day/night and seasons but it doesn't change the miracle of that moment when the dawn breaks across the sky. That sliver of light soon becomes a slice of life as birds begin to chirp declaring His handiwork and a new beginning to the day. There is nothing quite like it. It is at this moment of the day when the concept of this verse is most evident. Everything in creation holds its breath for one moment in awe as the light created, the spoken word of the Life-Light streams across the sky. Let there Be Light. When you are walking in a dark place of life seeking a glimpse of promise/hope/light, the tiniest of lights and the edge of promise urge you on towards hope. My favorite part of this verse is the promise-the darkness could not put it out! This is our eternal hope. It doesn't matter what comes our way-there is hope. No matter how grim the situation looks, there is hope. The night may come with aches and pains but there is always Light/Hope/Promise for though the darkness tries to hide it, there is always a ray, a glimmer or a glimpse. There is always Hope. Everything was created through Him. Not one thing came into being without Him including that darkness. He is the all. He is the source. He is the eternally present Life. What came was Life. Jesus. The Son which outshines the sun. The Light that shimmers, blazes and speaks is the Life. He and only He outlasts. There is no battery needed although staying plugged into Him and charging up is the way we stay encouraged and engaged. He doesn't require us, nor depend on us, but He walks with us and loves to hear our praises. His plans and purposes are above ours and far beyond what we can fathom, yet He cares for us in the smallest details. A friend posted yesterday that she got an alert on her ring that there was activity on the front porch of the house they just moved out of early in the morning yesterday. She clicked on the photo to realize it was a fire on her front porch. Immediately she called 911, but the fire consumed the home. She had decided to move only weeks before. She just felt it in her spirit and listened. No one and nothing was in the house when it caught ablaze. God kept her and her family despite the trials of cancer that they are currently facing. She sees it and knows it. No matter how wild your storm may seem or how overwhelming the waves crashing against you, He is still Light and you are still His. His Light-Life lives and breathes in you. Take heart. His purpose will come about. His truth will be revealed and you will be okay. Start looking for that glimmer of Light no matter how dark it seems, for it is there. The Light is there. The Life is there. The Promise is there. The Hope is there. For the Life-Light blazed out of the darkness; the darkness could not put it out! There is hope, so hold on. God has sent me here to tell you there is Hope! Darkness will not win! Disease/cancer does not win! Death doesn't win! Storms do not win! Challenging times do not last! Hope wins! The darkness can not put out The Light! Look to Him for He is here shining through your darkest moments. There is Hope!

God makes everything come out right;
he puts victims back on their feet.
He showed Moses how he went about his work,
opened up his plans to all Israel.
God is sheer mercy and grace;
not easily angered, he's rich in love.
He doesn't endlessly nag and scold,
nor hold grudges forever.
He doesn't treat us as our sins deserve,
nor pay us back in full for our wrongs.
As high as heaven is over the earth,
so strong is his love to those who fear him.
And as far as sunrise is from sunset,
he has separated us from our sins.
As parents feel for their children,
God feels for those who fear him.
He knows us inside and out,
keeps in mind that we're made of mud.
Men and women don't live very long;
like wildflowers they spring up and blossom,
But a storm snuffs them out just as quickly,
leaving nothing to show they were here.
God's love, though, is ever and always,
eternally present to all who fear him,
Making everything right for them and their children
as they follow his Covenant ways
and remember to do whatever he said.

Psalms 103:6-18

Back Right!

It seems like years that I have been living in a place of limbo but it has been only months. The place of the unknown stretches sometimes into an interminable place of waiting. It is in this place that God's faithfulness anchors us so much. The confidence stated by David in this Psalms song is echoed in our hearts in this waiting place. When transitions and life change impacts you, because it will, it is good to have a staying place. A staying place is a place of ultimate confidence that one can rest in through the ups and downs, ins and outs of life. God's love is a staying place. David describes it so poignantly in this passage. Sheer mercy and grace-as in, we can see His blessings and grace in our everyday moments. Not easily angered and rich in love which is described as not nagging nor scolding endlessly nor holding grudges, nor treatment as we deserve, nor paybacks for our wrongs but rather a light gentle rain, a warm hug, a pat on the head/back or just a place to blossom. God's love is a place of rest, confidence and knowing. He knows us. He loves us. Oh, how He loves us. He works to make all things right for us even while we are too busy in our lives. God makes everything come out right! This is the promise, the anchor, and the confidence of His love. God's love is ever and always, eternally present to all who fear Him, making everything right for us and our children as we follow in His ways. He will bring everything back right. If your world is upended and you are caught in a waiting place, have confidence in His anchoring love. The wind may screech, your boat may rock, the waves may wash over you instilling fear and seemingly overwhelming amounts of water may try to drown you but hold to His anchoring love and His promise. He knows you and loves you. He has you and He will bring everything back to you as He has promised. Our confidence is in that He has never failed. As parents feel for their children, so God feels for us. He knows us inside out. He knows our making, beginnings and endings. He knows us. This is our confidence. He will put things back right. Rest in Him!

Now God has us where he wants us, with all the time in this world and the next to shower grace and kindness upon us in Christ Jesus. Saving is all his idea, and all his work. All we do is trust him enough to let him do it. It's God's gift from start to finish! We don't play the major role. If we did, we'd probably go around bragging that we'd done the whole thing! No, we neither make nor save ourselves. God does both the making and saving. He creates each of us by Christ Jesus to join him in the work he does, the good work he has gotten ready for us to do, work we had better be doing.

Ephesians 2: 7-10

Grace Shower!

The Perseid Meteor Shower has been breathtaking the last couple of nights. Shooting stars and sparkling stardust all around reminds us that we are so insignificant and yet He loves us. The word shower means to rain down upon and Paul in his words to the church at Ephesus reminds us that it is all about God. God has us right where He wants us. Reliant on Him, complete dependence gives Him to have all the time in the world to shower grace and kindness on us. Saving was His idea and His work. The stars in the heavens, all His handiwork. The timing of everything, all His. All we have to do is trust Him enough to let Him do it. Just trust that His gift and provision is enough. We don't have to be in control but we must know that He is in control. He did the making of all our eyes can see and He is in the saving business where He sends us out in His authority declaring He is enough and He is. We just must walk in it and be about His business allowing Him to work the details out. He has created a good work for each of us to be busy doing. It is a good work He does through Christ Jesus who dwells in us by His Spirit. I am not a fan of walking in the rain as it is cold and wet but when it has been hot, steamy and miserable outside, walking into the rain is a blessing. We need to embrace the shower of His kindness and grace, hover in His umbrella of love and be blessed by His constancy in our lives. We need to understand that His love is so far above what we think or can imagine and His depth of love for us is filled with so much that the Earth is filled with His goodness. He has us in His hand showered in goodness, kindness, love, beauty and grace. Our role is to look up and trust in His love. His grace is enough, His goodness is enough, His faithfulness is enough...He is enough. Look up!

"Are you tired? Worn out? Burned out on religion? Come to me. Get away with me and you'll recover your life. I'll show you how to take a real rest. Walk with me and work with me—watch how I do it. Learn the unforced rhythms of grace. I won't lay anything heavy or ill-fitting on you. Keep company with me and you'll learn to live freely and lightly."

Matthew 11:28-30

Recover Life!

Giants seem to have trampled the grass in my life lately but they overlooked the pebbles under their feet and I am picking them up to put in my slingshot of God's word! I am refusing to take on heavy burdens and I am choosing to re-cover my life and walk in the unforced rhythms of His grace instead. I am claiming the promise that if I am tired and worn out, I can get away with God and recover. I have often felt like God allowed things too much for me to be put upon me and then I realized that He didn't put these burdens on me, I did. I made the choices that added too much to my day. I made the choice to take on the extra then got overwhelmed. There are things that have happened which have not been my choice but at any point, I can choose to just BE in Him. I can put it all away and soak into Him so that His life soaks into me. I can rest in His presence and take on His peace with His presence. I can find His rhythm of grace just by taking time in Him. Walk with Him. Work with Him. Watch how He moves. Learn to live freely and lightly in Him. This is how to recover LIFE!

All praise to the God and Father of our Master, Jesus the Messiah! Father of all mercy! God of all healing counsel! He comes alongside us when we go through hard times, and before you know it, he brings us alongside someone else who is going through hard times so that we can be there for that person just as God was there for us. We have plenty of hard times that come from following the Messiah, but no more so than the good times of his healing comfort—we get a full measure of that, too.

2 Corinthians 1:3-5

Full Measure!

Someone I care about is sick, in the hospital, struggling with illness, and has a burden too large to bear. Somedays this is me. Some Days it is a friend or loved one. Some Days it is another person who just needs to know we care. Hard times can define us. Places of downtime and struggles can show our character like no other because these are the training grounds. These are the places where we look to others and take care of them in their struggle. This passage starts with praise despite the struggle because it is in the praise that the struggle loses its power. Walking around the walls like at Jericho is the struggle but it isn't what brought the wall down. It was the shout of praise. The marching and doing, the standing and waiting are a part of the struggle. The prayer and the reading, the intense conversations with God all lead us to the victory of praise. If the praise is only had after the victory, then why have the cheerleaders. The praise drives the victory! Full measures are not limited to us because of our lives. Full measures are available always but we often stop at a partial. We pray believing but stop at declaring victory. The walls don't fall before the praise. They fall because of the praise. The trial may seem long and never-ending. It may look insurmountable but I am telling you that His faithfulness is still real and we can have confidence that He doesn't fail. I am sure that as the Israelites walked around that wall trudging day after day, they were mouthy and disgruntled not understanding the point. There were the priests and the encouraging ones who were constantly trying to uplift but let's be real. In about a million people, there were a lot of grumblers who just couldn't see the point in praying again in an impossible situation. There were the naysayers who kept talking about what a waste of time it all was. There were the skeptics, the whiners, the problematic people but there were also those who kept the vibe going. The believing had to overcome the naysayers and keep the faith. Faith is walking when you cannot see the purpose yet. Faith requires doing despite your doubt, fears and frustration. Faith has to be walked out and God wants us to walk along with those who are tired and weary to encounter them and encourage them so they do not falter or fail. The walking faith gets hard when those around you only see the impossible. Be a cheerleader for another. Come alongside and encourage someone else despite your own struggles because that is where the victory of praise comes in. His promises still stand but the walls will fall with the shout of praise. Get the praise revved up. Get ready to shout the walls down because the faith walking is shaking the foundations. There is purpose in the walking because it shakes that foundation so much that when that shout of praise comes from you, the walls will collapse and then the spoils of victory will be seen. Stir up the spirit of praise in you even while you are weary. You may have walked until you feel like you cannot go another step, but take one more, then one more and begin to stir up that song of praise, that shout of victory that will bring down the walls. Walk that faith then shout that praise! These walls will fall and the full measure of good times and healing comfort will be yours! God hears you walking your Jericho! The 7th day is coming-the day of praise! Keep walking and keep encouraging! Keep praising and keep believing! Most of all, keep stirring that shout of praise and remember that the shout of praise is what brings down the wall!

When the host tasted the water that had become wine (he didn't know what had just happened but the servants, of course, knew), he called out to the bridegroom, "Everybody I know begins with their finest wines and after the guests have had their fill brings in the cheap stuff. But you've saved the best till now!"

John 2:9-10

The Best!

Freshness is best. New flavor and zest. I am not an expert in culture of the day but I can picture this event as the crowd is there and they are running low on drinks. I am not getting into the debate on whether the wine was alcoholic or just a juice because that isn't what God has shared with me today. Please look at this verse for this nugget of truth. The host has no idea that a miracle has occurred nor did it matter to him. His remarks are simply viewpoint but they matter because the servants knew. They knew and probably were quaking in their hearts, for to them Jesus was just a man. They had used washing water...the jars that were filled with water to wash feet with and they had just served this to the host-the authority in the room. Obviously it is up to the bridegroom to furnish the beverages in this time and place because the host comments to the bridegroom that the best is now! Everybody I know, he says...this means in all his experiences, he has always seen people to give their best first then settle for the lesser. The servants know this is exactly what happened. They know that the bridegroom had not provided enough for the party but the host only comments on his experience. Why does this matter? Jesus had not wanted to perform this miracle but had done so at His mother's wish. He had not endeavored to make this happen but His mother knew what He could do and she placed her trust in Him and her trust was so contagious that the servants followed her wishes also. These servants risked their lives because they listened to Jesus at the word of His mother. Women didn't have authority in this culture and time so this is even more remarkable. Jesus performed this first documented miracle through the wish or prayer, if you will, of His mother because He loved her. He was obeying His Father's commandment to honor His mother. He did above and beyond the expected and the servants who risked it all did so because they believed in Mary's conviction. Often we get overwhelmed in our circumstances and we need someone else to stand in the gap, say the prayer, believe in faith and even be there through our circumstances. Often, we don't even know that someone is standing for us and doing this. I have no idea why this particular thing mattered to Mary but it did. She cared and she stood in the gap for this bridegroom. She knew with all her heart that Jesus would do as she asked. It never crossed her mind that He wouldn't, despite His words previously, because she was convinced of who He was. It was her faith, her conviction, her belief that made the connection to the best. It wasn't settling. It wasn't: I cannot do anything else so I will pray. It was: do what Jesus says because He will make a way. It was complete conviction and faith despite the circumstances of the situation. Jesus used what was available to bring about the absolute best because of her conviction. His mind was moved, His heart was changed because of her faith. He used the plain and undesired to become the best. He used the action of the servants and the washing water to become the BEST! They began to walk in conviction because Mary's faith was contagious. They followed Jesus' instructions as she said because her faith in Him was so palpable that they were convinced to risk it all. I see this again and again in scripture. It is the Faith action that brings the Best. The Best is Yet to Come. Jesus is returning for His bride and the marriage supper is being prepared. He has invited His people to prepare for this feast and He has the Best prepared. Meanwhile, we are His servants here to encourage others that His best is The Best there is in life. We need to quit acting like prayer is the smallest thing we can do and realize it is the most important thing we can do. We need to have faith that we can say to others, "Do as He commands you and The Best is yet to come". His best is The best. He has saved His Best for you. You just have to pick up that "washing water" and begin to pour it in faith. You have to take that simple prayer and endow it with the knowledge that He provides the Best through His word. Walk it out! He has good things in store for us, in fact, it is The Best!

During the time he was in Jerusalem, those days of the Passover Feast, many people noticed the signs he was displaying and, seeing they pointed straight to God, entrusted their lives to him. But Jesus didn't entrust his life to them. He knew them inside and out, knew how untrustworthy they were. He didn't need any help in seeing right through them.

John 2:23-25

Trustworthy!

Are we trustworthy? Could Jesus entrust His life to us? I honestly have never examined this aspect in my life before because I always heard from a young age that with salvation, Christ lives in me and dwells in me. Today as God led me to this place of scripture, He keeps tugging on me to be what He desires. People of the day trusted Jesus because they saw evidence in His life that He was who He said He was, so they entrusted Him with their lives. That's powerful as they lived in a time of unrest and adversity as a nation that was in Roman captivity. But the scriptures go on to say that Jesus didn't entrust them, because He knew them inside and out. He knew they were untrustworthy and didn't need help seeing that. This broke my heart as I, for the first time in my life, began to think, would Jesus see me as trustworthy with His life? This King of Glory who gave up everything for me, even His own life in sacrifice, knows me inside and out. What does He see in me? Does He see and know that I am trustworthy so that He can entrust His very being to me or am I like those who walked with Him, trusting Him but being found wanting in my trustworthiness? What am I doing with Jesus? How much of our lives are we spending on the mortal, the flawed and the fading versus that which has no end? Whose ideas and marks are we carrying the flag for? What title or aegis do we bear? When people see us, do they see Jesus or do they see and hear mortal advice and earthly manner? What are we doing with Jesus? He can perform signs and wonders, but are we being used by Him to do that, or are we caught up in our day to day cares forgetting the Who He is? Can He entrust us with His life? Even those who walked closest to Him, day by day, abandoned Him when the walk got tough. They denied Him when the trials got hard. They betrayed Him for riches. They fell asleep when He called them to pray. What am I doing about Jesus? Am I trustworthy? Can He entrust Himself to me?

Those who think they can do it on their own end up obsessed with measuring their own moral muscle but never get around to exercising it in real life. Those who trust God's action in them find that God's Spirit is in them—living and breathing God! Obsession with self in these matters is a dead end; attention to God leads us out into the open, into a spacious, free life. Focusing on the self is the opposite of focusing on God. Anyone completely absorbed in self ignores God, ends up thinking more about self than God. That person ignores who God is and what he is doing. And God isn't pleased at being ignored.

Romans 8:5-8

God Absorbed!

The counter was ruined! It had an ugly foggy color that was all scratched up. The beautiful shining midnight granite was now a cloudy, muddy mess. What happened? The sponge used to clean the counter had absorbed too much of other stuff and now that filth was ingrained into the granite scarring it. All because of the sponge...the sponge had a hidden secret...it had absorbed rotten dirt from scrubbing potatoes and other substances then had not been properly cleansed. It took that filth into its fibers then when it was once again put into use, it released that filth onto the new surface scarring it. The granite will have to be stripped, cleaned and resurfaced now in order to restore it. All because of a dirty sponge that had absorbed what it was used to clean. Our lives are like a sponge. When we are soaked and stoked in ourselves, we scrub and take in so much of the world around us and the filth that says have it your way, that we absorb it into our very fibers. We become self absorbed. Then the time comes to be used, we soak in The Living Water and we have the cleansing power of the Word loaded as we approach the midnight surface. Now as the scrubbing begins, suddenly, we are not releasing only the Word and Living Water but we are letting out our own self-absorbed filth as well, mixing it with the Word and the Living Water, scarring the surface of the ministry God has given us. We have allowed that soaking And absorption of self to start releasing that selfish pride and ambition instead of being fully used by God. I know this is a harsh lesson today as I am feeling it. God is calling us to be pure and cleansed so that we may be fully absorbed in Him and not stained with selfish ambition and greed. In Romans, we see this. The author says through the anointing that those who think they can do it on their own, end up measuring their own abilities but never truly exercising the moral muscle of God. You see that when we are self absorbed, we cannot take in the truth of God into our fiber because we are too full of self. When we try to minister to others, too much of the stinky self gets mixed up with the truth and everything becomes muddy to others. The only way to truly work in God's Spirit and God's actions is to be cleansed completely of self. Those who trust God's action in them find that the living, breathing Spirit of God is in them. How to check, soak in God's word, God's presence, God's anointing until the stench of selfish ambition is released into the Living Water and the fibers of your being are absorbed with Him. When it begins to be all about Him, then you have found the Actions of a Living, Breathing Spirit of God. God's spirit will not operate fully in a self absorbed person. Sure, even a dirty trick can be used to scour a surface but to bring beauty from ashes and miracles to life, it requires the God action of the God absorbed not the self absorbed. I encourage you to get alone with God and soak. Let Him begin to seep in and cleanse those hidden fibers of self. It isn't an easy process nor a quick one, but it is a process of seeing and feeling His living and breathing Spirit in you. Shut yourself in with Him for some soaking and cleaning as He renews the right Spirit in you.

Jesus said, "You're not listening. Let me say it again. Unless a person submits to this original creation—the 'wind-hovering-over-the-water' creation, the invisible moving the visible, a baptism into a new life—it's not possible to enter God's kingdom. When you look at a baby, it's just that: a body you can look at and touch. But the person who takes shape within is formed by something you can't see and touch—the Spirit—and becomes a living spirit.

John 3:5-6

Listening Truth!

"You're not listening!" I heard that statement several times today and each time it resulted in a disagreement of some kind. Then I opened The Word and here it is again. Must be something God is trying to say to me. Jesus was addressing a ruler, a teacher, and an authority in the times. This man had just argued with Jesus when He explained that you must be born again. The man could not grasp what was being taught. So Jesus told him that he wasn't listening and he patiently restated it again. Submission to the Spirit over the flesh is the key to the kingdom. There is no way to enter God's kingdom in the flesh. It is a spiritual kingdom. We live in such an evidence based world that we do not truly grasp this easily. So Jesus explained it as a baby with flesh. We see the body which we can touch but the person that takes shape within is formed by the Spirit which we cannot see nor touch. We assume this is the visible over the invisible but it is really the opposite. We spend a lot of time focusing on the earthly and the tangible but we fail to see the intangible and put the same effort into that part of our lives. We wake and prepare for school or work, we prepare for our entertainment events but we are lax when it comes to preparing and taking the time required to listen in His presence. We rush through the prayer to get to the meal. We rush through our time at church, our time in the Word, our time with Him to get on to the tangible, forgetting that the invisible is what matters. Are you listening? Unless a person submits and yields their life completely to this original creation-the spirit-then they miss the point of existence. Legacy is important and leaving behind things for our families is important but it is more important that we spend time in the legacy of the spirit. There are no grandchildren in the Spirit. The legacy is only what we do to demonstrate the full love and dedication to the Spirit. It isn't about convincing others but rather quietly leading others. Too often this is a place of struggle for many including me. When the invisible Spirit of God is moving and we in our flesh rush over it in a big hurry to make things happen, we miss out on the things He has. I think of the promise of the rainbow and how it still remains today. The promise hasn't changed. God's word hasn't changed. God hasn't changed. The invisible and intangible hasn't changed. He still resides deep within us in our spirit. There is a God sized hole in each of us that can only be filled by His Spirit and it is what leads us into the eternal. When we focus more on the tangible and spend all our efforts on the tangible, we miss that still small voice beckoning us into the eternal. What truth are we listening to? Jesus says He is the Truth, The Way and the Life and no man comes to the Father but through Him. Are we listening?

What I'm getting at, friends, is that you should simply keep on doing what you've done from the beginning. When I was living among you, you lived in responsive obedience. Now that I'm separated from you, keep it up. Better yet, redouble your efforts. Be energetic in your life of salvation, reverent and sensitive before God. That energy is God's energy, an energy deep within you, God himself willing and working at what will give him the most pleasure.

Philippians 2:13

Redoubled Effort!

Responsive obedience is a phrase that simply means to keep listening and doing as God wills us to do despite our circumstances. I have found it is easier to say But...I would but....as we add an excuse to why we are not doing as we know to do. Recently I asked someone to help me with something and they responded that they "might try" which is essentially a No. They had no intention of trying thus, the might. Paul instructed the Philippians and us through the Word to be energized in our life of salvation and to be reverent and sensitive before God. Until I saw this photo filmed from an airplane by a pilot, I had no idea that a rainbow was an unending circle. I always assumed it was only an arc but that is just the part I perceived. Having the energy of God means going above and beyond. Not only doubling but redoubling our efforts means working four times as hard through His energy. Keep on. I know we get tired walking and waiting. I know it gets exhausting but He said keep going. Keep doing what you know to do and not only that but do it with redoubled effort in reverence and sensitivity towards God so that He may pour His energy into us and work into us what He desires in His perfect will. When it looks impossible, remember He is the God of the impossible. Just keep going, looking for the promise and knowing it is more than double and redoubled what we expect. We only see part. Soon we shall see all.

My dear, dear friends, if God loved us like this, we certainly ought to love each other. No one has seen God, ever. But if we love one another, God dwells deeply within us, and his love becomes complete in us—perfect love!

1 John 4:11-12

Perfect Love!

What is love? Some describe it as emotion. Some see it as an action. Some fault it for failures and others saddle it with false expectations. Love is God and God is love. They are synonymous because everyone that loves is born of God for God is love. The issue is understanding what perfect love is. Disney and society have tried to describe love as an accidental relationship that results in lust of the flesh or a magical emotion that one cannot control. Love is not that. Love is the Spirit of God inhabited in the flesh reaching out to others despite their failures. Love is so much more than just a simple emotional feeling or response. It is an abiding. God dwells deeply within us when we allow His Spirit to inhabit us and as His love fills us, it bursts out of us into the world around us allowing us to love large. When His love has free reign, unstifled, within us, it becomes perfect. All the romance movies and Princess stories try to depict a perfect love but miss the mark because they do not understand that love is what happens after the fairytale "The End". Love is the waking/sleeping and all the in between choices. Perfect Love is in the choosing. The scripture says, if we love one another, meaning it is a choice. Choosing to love allows love to grow. Choosing when it is hard. Choosing when it means forgiving. Choosing when you don't agree. Choosing when life gives us lemons. Choosing to walk in His love because we don't feel it. Emotions fade. Emotions are like roller coasters and are affected by mood, flesh, sickness, lack of sleep, stress, etc. but love is not an emotion. It is more than an action or feeling. It is choosing to allow God to move through us into the life of another despite the circumstances. Love isn't fickle. It doesn't go away when someone does wrong. Love is a choice just like doing right in a hard situation is a choice. It is a skill that we exercise like faith in the hard times so that it stretches us and allows God's Spirit to move fully in us. Love has a name. Its name is Jesus. In each situation and circumstance, if we choose what Jesus would do, ask Him for His Wisdom, His heart, His guidance, then and only then can we walk in true Perfect love which casts out all fear and opens the door to Eternal Hope in Him. This is a simple choice that uses our actions to walk it out. Perfect love is within our grasp and we don't have to have the perfect spouse to attain it. Perfect love is in Jesus and He supplies all we need. Love needs to reset in our lives so that we begin to walk fully in the choice of love and not judgment nor criticism nor emotion. Love is God and God is love. The more of Him one has, the more love one has to share. If you are feeling stretched today, thank God because He is preparing you to love more. If you are in an impossible place of emotion, give it to Him so He can fill that void of empty pain/hurt with His loving presence. Begin to walk in love and not in emotion. Choose love. Choose God. Choose this day to serve.

Watch what God does, and then you do it, like children who learn proper behavior from their parents. Mostly what God does is love you. Keep company with him and learn a life of love. Observe how Christ loved us. His love was not cautious but extravagant. He didn't love in order to get something from us but to give everything of himself to us. Love like that.
Ephesians 5:1

Proper Behavior!

Confession: I used this picture for two reasons, one, she is my grand-dog and I knew her picture would get my kids to look; two, training a puppy who has been abandoned to love and trust again takes extravagant love and patience which is exactly what God demonstrates to us and says we are to do for others. This verse says to watch what God does and then do it like children (or dogs) who have learned proper behavior through training from their parents. My daughter-in-law often tells me how grateful she is that I trained my boys to clean up after themselves and to do house-hold chores as well as outdoors activities because it matters in a marriage. This behavior came from training by me and by example from their dad. We are to learn to love like God because He trains us in His word and in His actions for us to love like that. This sweetheart puppy was abandoned on the porch steps of my son's house by her momma who was a stray. That momma dog likely did it out of love because she knew that her puppy would have a much better life there. There, she is pampered and loved, taught and trained. She has had a lot of adjustment to this new life for sure and some of that has been hard but she is loved and instructed. The more she keeps company with her new family, the more she learns the rhythm and patterns of their love and devotion so that this can be her pattern also. God's love is much more than our love for our pets or even our children. God's love is extraordinary as He didn't love to get anything from us. He just loved and that love so deep and true found its way to become more in us and through us. God desires that same action and being in us so that as His love fills us, it takes on the same possibilities as His love in His son. The instructions here are to keep company with God and learn a life of love. In other words, love like Jesus, sacrificially. Love like God, constantly and consistently. Love like that by learning His love patterns. Love is mentioned hundreds of times in the Bible because God wants us to operate and move, grow, have our being inside His fullness of love. His love is our daily bread and our nightly rest. His love comes with discipline and authority. His love has responsibilities and rewards. His love is more than an emotion or action. It is a living, breathing, presence representing Him in our lives. How do we love like God? We watch what God does and then we love like that-Not cautiously but extravagantly. We don't do to get, we love in order to experience His love fully. I imagine sweet Julie will end up as spoiled as her sister Holly. Although they do not have the same birth mothers nor are they from the same breed, they have ended up in a household of love. Love breeds love. Love is of God and everyone who loves like that is born of God for He who loves God knows love. Challenging myself today to love like that!

Anyone who meets a testing challenge head-on and manages to stick it out is mighty fortunate. For such persons loyally in love with God, the reward is life and more life. James 1:12

Testing Challenge!

We all want to be mighty fortunate and gain great reward. We are wired to want reward and love. This heat has been a challenge to endure for many reasons and although we have been shattering heat records set years ago daily, we are so fortunate. We have AC. I was looking at the heat records and thinking about all the years of record heat with no AC, no ice, nothing cold to cool you, then I realized that we are very blessed. Lots of tests come our way and sometimes we feel bowed down low by them but James encourages us to meet these challenges head on. He says that those who persist in loyal love of God through the testing challenges of life reap the rewards of life. Life eternal is not life in this mortal. Yesterday I found out that a dear person to me was suddenly called away to eternity. Oh, how it shocked my soul and how I grieved for her family as it was so quick. Tomorrow isn't promised. Tomorrow may bring the biggest fight of your life or the biggest victory. Tomorrow may bring death, grief or triumph, but whatever comes our way and no matter how tired we are, our source is in Him. Loyal love is the cheat sheet to the testing challenge. When we are down, God picks us up. Start counting the blessings such as AC that we have through God's love. If you start looking for the good, then you will find it in the testing challenge as you meet it head on. Then and only then, you will stick it out to the end where the reward of eternal life exists. Our challenges might be 15 days, 7 months, or 26 years long. For the Israelites it was 40 long hard years but God was with them the entire time. Don't give up on the battle. God has given us the victory, we just have to meet the challenge in faith surrounded by His love in Us.

Meanwhile, the moment we get tired in the waiting, God's Spirit is right alongside helping us along. If we don't know how or what to pray, it doesn't matter. He does our praying in and for us, making prayer out of our wordless sighs, our aching groans. He knows us far better than we know ourselves, knows our pregnant condition, and keeps us present before God. That's why we can be so sure that every detail in our lives of love for God is worked into something good.
Romans 8:28

Wordless Sighs!

I heard the sigh of his very first breath and I heard that sigh of relief in his voice yesterday as he had something he has worked toward become a reality. You may not see the photo clearly behind this scripture but it is another moment of satisfied sigh as my daughter in law completed getting her room ready for her first day of teaching!! We all have them-wordless sighs! They are the breath of God's Spirit making prayer from our wordless moments of sorrow to celebration. He takes our aching groans and turns them into hallelujahs. He knows our ins and outs. Our very situations of desperation and depth of sorrow pull His heart strings of love toward us as He wraps His strong arms of love around us. It doesn't matter if you don't have the words to say, He does. His is The Word. He knows us and that is why we can be confident that no matter what comes our way, He is at work in all the details in our lives of love for God as He works it all out for our good. I have been heavy weighted with several issues until I realized that He never intended me to carry these burdens alone. My husband tells me often to quit trying to carry or do things alone because he stays concerned about my health. He knows I have limits. God isn't limited. When we are completely exhausted and worn, slap out from the battles of life, God's Spirit is there right with us, helping us. Wordless sighs of wonder, grief, joy, sorrow, celebration, excitement, surprise, and exhaustion all travel to Him as prayers. If you are out of words, out of fight, out of energy and emotion, just out of it all, sigh His name deeply-He will meet you there. There is nothing too big or too small for Him. He knows you. He knows exactly what you are going through. Let it go in a deep wordless sigh to Him with your heart focused on who He is and He will hear your wordless sighs and aching groans. He is enough. Let it Go! He has it. Breathe in deeply-Let it all go to Him in a deep breath-filled sigh. Then rest and lean in as He works it all out for your good.

Hallelujah! Thank God! Pray to him by name! Tell everyone you meet what he has done! Sing him songs, belt out hymns, translate his wonders into music! Honor his holy name with Hallelujahs, you who seek God. Live a happy life! Keep your eyes open for God, watch for his works; be alert for signs of his presence. Remember the world of wonders he has made, his miracles, and the verdicts he's rendered— O seed of Abraham, his servant, O child of Jacob, his chosen.

Psalms 105:1

Happy Life!

Live a happy life! It's a choice. Circumstances may bow you down and days may come that make you fret. Times may get tough but happiness is still a choice. If you keep your eyes open for God and watch for His works and for signs of His presence then your mind will be focused on Him and not on those things that weigh on you. Mindless pursuits, drugs including alcohol, and other things that distract us from the truth, mask what is True Happiness. True Happiness isn't found in having wealth, possessions, and all your dreams as reality. True happiness is found in the joy that only He can bring. The psalmist reminds us to remember the world our wondrous God has made along with the miracles seen and unseen. Today as I looked through my sons' baby books, I was once again struck with the awesomeness of who He is and what He does. I was once again reminded of His creative nature and His infinite goodness in the simple concept that is so complex in reproduction and birth. The psalmists say to sing Him songs, belt out hymns and translate His wonders into music which is what I hear the birds doing and the wind and the trees as with all of nature. I thank God for my children and all their family. I want to shout from the rooftops of all the wonders He has done for us through their lives. Hallelujah God! I call you by Name and thank you for your goodness for you have done great things. Life may not be perfect. It certainly has its challenges and trials but I am so grateful for all the good that He has done for me.

My response is to get down on my knees before the Father, this magnificent Father who parcels out all heaven and earth. I ask him to strengthen you by his Spirit—not a brute strength but a glorious inner strength—that Christ will live in you as you open the door and invite him in. And I ask him that with both feet planted firmly on love, you'll be able to take in with all followers of Jesus the extravagant dimensions of Christ's love. Reach out and experience the breadth! Test its length! Plumb the depths! Rise to the heights! Live full lives, full in the fullness of God.
Ephesians 3:16

Reach Out!

In this passage of scripture, Paul speaks about the reach of God's love. He encourages us to experience it. This puzzled me at first because I had always read it with love as an emotion. When I began to understand that Love was God and God was Love, the perspective on this verse changed. Emotions come and go but God's love lasts infinitely. There is a reason that love is compared to hope and faith because they are intertwined. If our faith is built on earthly things that fail us, then our hope will also falter and we will begin to doubt love exists. If we base our faith on God's infinite Love, then we always have hope because He cannot fail and we will always feel His love surround us even when we are choosing to be unhappy with our circumstances and choices. Happiness is a choice that is based on who we are rather than what we have. The corporate world thrives on finding the "happiness" factor because they know that everyone craves that from the poorest person in poverty to the millionaires. Happiness is not attainable through money, drugs nor power just like love is not attainable through divisive means nor manipulation. Sex is not love although the world tries to sell it that way. Happiness is not riches though many believe that. Fulfillment is not power in the government although many think that is the means. Strength is not in physical manifestation but in spirit. Inner strength with Christ alive in you allows you to firmly plant your feet in His love with confidence that no matter what the circumstances that surround you, He is working them out for your good. Hope in Him is based in the Faith of knowing who He is. This is why Paul says that we take in the extravagant dimensions of His love and explore it. This is why He says to reach out and experience the complexity and completeness. He says to experience its breadth, test its length, plumb the depths and rise to the heights by living full lives in the fullness of God. Too many times we walk under the weight of our circumstances instead of rising above them in confidence that He is in control. Too many times we allow our situations to dictate our future rather than realizing that He has a plan for us that far exceeds ours. I am as guilty as many for failing to see His truth because the place I am in seems overwhelming but then I remember who He is. He isn't limited by me or my circumstances. His love doesn't stop because my financial means are tight. His infinite mercy hasn't failed because I did. He is larger than what we can imagine and far greater than we believe. Our finite minds cannot take in the whole but we can dive deep and still never reach the depths of His love for us. Today is a day of exploration. Test and see that His love is beyond what you imagine. Live a full life in Him today. Choose happiness because you know no matter what, He has great things in store for you!

The word that saves is right here,
as near as the tongue in your mouth,
as close as the heart in your chest.
It's the word of faith that welcomes God to
go to work and set things right for us. This is
the core of our preaching. Say the welcoming
word to God—"Jesus is my Master"—
embracing, body and soul, God's work of
doing in us what he did in raising Jesus from
the dead. That's it. You're not "doing"
anything; you're simply calling out to God,
trusting him to do it for you. That's salvation.
With your whole being you embrace God
setting things right, and then you say it, right
out loud: "God has set everything right
between him and me!"

Romans 10:8-10

Right Here!

One of my favorite all time songs is "He is as Close as the Mention of His Name" The Word, Jesus, is right here, right now as close as the tongue in your mouth or the heart in your chest. It is as simple as mentioning His name to activate the faith that welcomes God to go to work and set things right for us. Simply saying, Jesus is my Master, and embracing with your whole body and soul, God's work of salvation through the selfless giving of His son and raising Him from the dead, you activate the Word of Faith. It isn't hard work. It is a simplistic belief that He is who He says He is. With your whole being, you embrace God and let Him have it. We simply let it all go into His capacity. Just simply call out to God and trust Him to do it, whatever it may be, for you. Simply let Him have all the pain, all the stress, all the struggle, etc. Let Him take it and give you peace instead. We carry so much within ourselves. We worry, fret, scheme, plan, fret, cry, scream, etc. We allow our emotions to dictate the truth rather than simple trust. Why? We are emotional creatures. We allow our desires and thoughts to get ahead of God so often because we do not feel that He is moving quickly enough. We get overwhelmed and we jump ahead of where He is. The truth is that God has provided us a way of escape from the traps we make for ourselves and it is as simple as whispering His name in faith believing that He has all things under His control. A lack of faith is a lack of trust in who He says He is. The miracle we need is already in the making and on its way. It simply takes the act of faith to reach out to Jesus and say, here it is Lord. Whatever you want to happen, I will trust that you know what you are doing. It is yours. It always has been and I acknowledge it now that you are truly Master of all. Take this situation Lord. Take my life, my work, my home, my every moment and make it yours. I lean into your safekeeping and rest in your presence. All I am is yours. All I have is yours. Then let it be. He will guide you and walk you through it. He is right here-as close as the mention of His name-Jesus.

"I've told you these things for a purpose: that my joy might be your joy, and your joy wholly mature. This is my command: Love one another the way I loved you. This is the very best way to love. Put your life on the line for your friends. You are my friends when you do the things I command you. I'm no longer calling you servants because servants don't understand what their master is thinking and planning. No, I've named you friends because I've let you in on everything I've heard from the Father.

John 15:11-15

Wholly Mature!

What is wholly mature joy? It is joy that cannot be stolen by your circumstances. Maturity takes confidence and training. Training to be joy filled is a process. It is learning to love, not as an emotion but as an action, when someone deserves it and when they don't. It is recognizing the need for help and hope when others are hurting and moving into that place of need despite your own place of need. When Jesus revealed His plans and purpose to the disciples and then to us through the written word, He revealed Himself-the epitome of Love. Love suffers long and is kind. Love never gives up. Never lets go. Never gives in. Walking in God's active love is the key to being joy filled. I can say that I am still in training to acquire mature joy. How do I know this? Because my circumstances do not necessarily dictate happiness but I am faced with the choice to walk in defeat/frustration or to walk in confidence of His love that no matter what happens, He is in control and that He is working all things out for my good because He loves me with an everlasting love. Making that choice to choose happiness and confidence in His love is the training ground of mature joy. Mature Joy means you learn to put Jesus first, Others next and Yourself last as this spells JOY! Joy isn't about having a perfect life. Joy isn't about everything working on time and in your favor immediately. Joy isn't about not having problems. Joy is about choosing to love in action, word and deed despite your circumstances. Mature Joy means making the right choice. Choosing to love others the way Christ Jesus loved us. Mature Joy walks in Peace. Mature Joy is filled with God's love. Mature Joy cannot be stolen or ripped away by circumstances. Mature Joy is a state of mind, heart and soul being one in commitment to the confidence of God's love. Mature Joy requires the love that puts your own happiness and fulfillment on the line for others but results in Joyful Peace. This Joy that I have wasn't given to me by my spouse, kids, parents, circumstances, job, career, or anything other than through my choice to walk in His confident Love. I could write volumes about trials, and my life would make a soap opera look tame for all the drama, but Joy is my choice. I choose His Love, His Joy, His Peace and I walk in it. For sure, I have my moments-ask my family...that is the development stage-the choosing stage of becoming Mature in Joy. So today I challenge you to choose Joy. No matter what today holds. Choose Joy. Perhaps today you can be like these roses in this photo, beautiful despite the snow. Blooming despite the ice. Fragrant despite the harshness. Choose Joy!

If your heart is broken, you'll find God right there; if you're kicked in the gut, he'll help you catch your breath. Psalms 34:18

Catch His Breath!

When my eldest son was little, he hated the wind blowing in his face as it took his breath and he would get so startled then scared and would cry and scream which then made it worse. We were so surprised that when his little brother was born, that same phenomenon fascinated him so much that he loved turning the blow dryer on in his face. He would turn the blow dryer towards himself, just so he could catch his breath, and he delighted in it. We all approach heartache differently. Some of us immediately turn inward in stress and get quiet, others yell and scream while some find their rhythm and ride the waves of heartache in a rush embracing the moment of pain knowing things will turn again. As I stood looking at this beautiful blue super-moon last night/early morning, I thought of the people in my life who were walking through trials, sorrow or pain right now and how we all approached it differently, yet, God is within each of us working something out for our good. The kick in the gut that has taken your breath away and tried to steal your joy is only temporary. He will help you catch your breath. He will deliver you from the impossible situation or the unbearable grief. He will lighten your load and He is there/here in the moment with you but you must lean in. As long as we try to do it in our own strength, we are going to struggle with catching our breath and we will truly feel the heartbreak but if we lean in, He shares the load and speaks peace in the midst. We are God breathed. The breath that fills our lungs from the very beginning of life, that sustains us until we are born is God breathed. He knew us from the moment of creation. He intimately formed us in our mother's wombs. We are sacred and special to Him. Uniquely His. Unique in ourselves. Step out into His love trusting that He is enough. He will help us catch our breaths no matter how big the gut punch nor how many times we got punched recently. I watched a show recently with my husband about George Foreman as he navigated the journey to God through boxing. He got punched down and out. It seemed that he was happiest in the world's eyes when he was living and operating in the angry man phase. Then upon his salvation, the struggle became real evident. The world didn't love him. They were entertained by him for a moment but forgot him quickly when he decided to live for Christ. Then he came back to boxing again and rose to the heights again, but this time with God by his side. Now, he has a platform for ministry on the world stage, because despite being sidelined and punched out, God gave him new breath and new life. Rise up like my son, Gabriel, confident that the air being stolen from you is being replaced with God breath. Embrace the breath taking moments in confidence. Trade the gut punch-lost breath-for one filled with purpose and love from God. Catch His breath! Catch His purpose! The moon is so beautiful that this took my breath away and God replaced it with His breath of assurance. He will not fail you. He is your breath. Breathe Him in.

"But there is another urgency before me now. I feel compelled to go to Jerusalem. I'm completely in the dark about what will happen when I get there. I do know that it won't be any picnic, for the Holy Spirit has let me know repeatedly and clearly that there are hard times and imprisonment ahead. But that matters little. What matters most to me is to finish what God started: the job the Master Jesus gave me of letting everyone I meet know all about this incredibly extravagant generosity of God.

Acts 20:22-24

Urgent Job!

Urgency! That is the feeling I have felt the last few weeks, like time is running out. The urgent need to complete a job given to me by God Himself is upon me. That job is to share His extraordinary forgiveness and extravagant mercy, grace and generosity with all that I meet. Paul too felt this urgency even though he also knew it meant hard times ahead for his own self. As I listened to others talk about their day-to-day struggles, I felt the pain of my own body, soul, and mind with all my struggles, then thought, this is why I have this sense of urgency. I am not feeling rushed by my job, but rather by my pending sense of Jesus' return. As I gazed upon the beautiful moon, I thought of the Revelation where the moon turns to blood. I thought of the signs of the times everywhere from scanning palms to get groceries now at Whole Foods to the cashless societal push. Times are winding down. The Earth is groaning with fires, earthquakes, hurricanes and famine, disease and pestilence. I look around and see prophecy being fulfilled with signs of the times everywhere. Like the song "Midnight Cry" says, I can almost hear that trumpet as Gabriel sounds the call. If I knew today was the day, who would I tell? Why am I waiting? Today could very well be that day. Do you know my Jesus? I would love to introduce you to this magnificent God who willingly laid down His life for you and even now is preparing a place for you in eternity. May I introduce you to my friend who is closer than a brother?

Jerusalem will be told:
"Don't be afraid.
Dear Zion,
don't despair.
Your God is present among you,
a strong Warrior there
to save you.
Happy to have you back, he'll
calm you with his love
and delight you with his songs.

Zephaniah 3:16-17

Strong Warrior!

Zion is Holiness Hill! It is a Hebrew word meaning City of Holiness or City of Refuge. It is metaphorically speaking, the place of peace and stability, safety and comfort. In Zephaniah, the Israelites have been in captivity and scattered. God speaks to them instructionally that He is bringing them back to Him in triumph and deliverance. He speaks to those who have battled and are weary as Jerusalem. I love to read this promise as mine for it is!

"Don't be afraid. Dear one, don't despair. Our God is present among us, a strong warrior here to save us. He is happy to welcome you back and He will calm you with His love and delight you with His songs." What a terrific promise! He is our warrior here to save us! I adore this photo of the Northern Lights because they look like the skirts of a bridal gown and remind me that soon He is coming to catch His bride away. I cannot imagine a more sacred or celebrated moment than the moment we reunite with Jesus. All the unexpected hardships will suddenly be made new and worthy. I cannot fathom anything better than to melt into His embrace but until then, He tells us His presence is with us as a strong warrior. I certainly do not know your circumstances but I do know the power of His name! I do not know your problems nor your victories but I do know that whatever they are, He is there in them with us. He is our strong warrior! He is our present help! He will calm you with His love and delight you with His songs. Take time to listen and hear Him calling sweetly. This strong warrior calls to your heart to walk into His arms of love, His strong embrace and to put fear aside for He is fighting on your behalf. Science doesn't hold Him. Politics don't impress Him. Technology doesn't fathom Him. There is nothing above Him or below Him that He cannot handle. He is our strong Warrior! He has us! He fights for us! He speaks peace to us. Don't be afraid! Don't despair! God has you and He is your strong warrior! Read it! Say it! Believe it! Hold to it! Delight in it! Sing it! Pray it! Walk in it!

Enter with the password: "Thank you!" Make yourselves at home, talking praise. Thank him. Worship him.

Psalms 100:4

Talking Praise!

Talking praise leads to walking praise! I remember when my son was little and he would get into trouble. I could hear him talking in his room, assuring himself of my love just as I had assured him. He would say, " I did something bad but she still loves me and because she loves me, she disciplines me but she still loves me." These are the words that I taught him. I told him he was valued and loved. Mistakes come with consequences but it doesn't lessen God's love for us even while we are in the pain of the consequences. A few days ago, I stepped out of my car onto a curb and ended up falling and injuring myself a lot. The pain has been severe and I have prayed believing that God is healing me as I know He loves me even while I live in these consequences of the accident. My body aches all over from the fall as it was a hard crash. I have chosen to count the blessings despite the pain. One thing I conquered through it was the fear of permanent paralysis with a fall. I didn't even realize I was living in that fear until I fell. The pain in my foot/leg and body hurts but my praise for the injury not being a permanent debilitation is real. I am so grateful that the fall was not a broken back or worse. Life has consequences for actions and accidents. We have a choice to enter into His presence with our consequences and despite our struggles. We can choose to walk in His truthful light of praise that casts a rainbow of promise through our storms. We can choose to have talking praise until we are ready to be walking in praise. We can thank Him despite our circumstances and because of His love even while we are in the throes of pain, hurt, disappointment or other. My son talked himself into understanding reality until he was able to understand the concept that my love would not change. God's love is enduring and constant. He is faithful and forever. It is our choice to enter into His presence and it only takes a simple password of "Thank you". If you start with thanking, you will soon be in, talking praise which leads to walking praise, which leads to miracles and wave walking despite the storm. Wave walking only comes from praise talking. It is the faith action that comes from knowing who He is. Make yourselves at home in His talking praise. Thank Him. Worship Him. Delight in Him. This is how the talking praise becomes the miracle. No matter what our circumstances, we have the choice to enter into His presence. Thank you Lord for giving this song to me. Thank you Lord for having my back. Thank you Lord for keeping me through these circumstances. Thank you Lord....

In a well-furnished kitchen there are not only crystal goblets and silver platters, but waste cans and compost buckets—some containers used to serve fine meals, others to take out the garbage. Become the kind of container God can use to present any and every kind of gift to his guests for their blessing.
2 Timothy 2:20-21

God Container!

What kind of container are you? This scripture picture contains a horsefly that is Huge! He has bothered me and my friends every day as we swim but today we were not swimming so he sat on the window waiting with no purpose. What is her purpose? So I did a little digging and discovered that horseflies must have blood to have their little ones and the bigger the horsefly, the closer they are to birthing. I understand her purpose now but I am not interested in me being her feast! God can use anything to be a container of His use but in this scripture, the author is telling us that we have a choice of what kind of container we want to become. We can be a container like a crystal goblet and silver platter that carries His love, kindness and everlasting mercy to others or we can be a waste basket that harbors the leftovers because we are choosing to not be the carrier but rather only the receiver. The verses surrounding this scripture say, "Fix this picture firmly in your mind: Jesus, descended from the line of David, raised from the dead. It's what you've heard from me all along. It's what I'm sitting in jail for right now—but God's Word isn't in jail! That's why I stick it out here—so that everyone God calls will get in on the salvation of Christ in all its glory. This is a sure thing: If we die with him, we'll live with him; If we stick it out with him, we'll rule with him; If we turn our backs on him, he'll turn his back on us; If we give up on him, he does not give up— for there's no way he can be false to himself. Meanwhile, God's firm foundation is as firm as ever, these sentences engraved on the stones: God knows who belongs to Him. Steer clear of evil, all you who name God as God." 2 Timothy 2:8-13, 19 MSG

You really need to read the whole chapter. You need to carry this yummy bread of life around to those you meet instead of only getting the morsel others are sharing. You need to choose to become the kind of container that can carry anything God wishes you to carry into wherever He sends you. Are you willing to dive into His word and become the servant of the Almighty to carry the fine meals to others or are you simply comfortable being the compost heap receiving only the morsels and repeating those to others? I challenge you. Be the fierce momma horsefly that goes after the head-the freshness to feed the children rather than the housefly that is happy with reused compost. Be the one that strikes out and becomes the silver serving tray reflecting His glory in the meal as you take in His bread of life and serve it to others. Quit settling for the cast off from others and begin to dive deep into His word and grow in His knowledge. Challenge yourself to get out into the highways and byways, sharing His feast with others. Step out into the gifts of the Spirit and be a crystal goblet that holds His new wine of the Spirit in tongues and interpretation. Stop being just the garbage bin and compost heap that takes in what others have cast off. God is God. "This is a sure thing: If we die with him, we'll live with him; If we stick it out with him, we'll rule with him; If we turn our backs on him, he'll turn his back on us; If we give up on him, he does not give up— for there's no way he can be false to himself. Meanwhile, God's firm foundation is as firm as ever, these sentences engraved on the stones: God knows who belongs to Him. Steer clear of evil, all you who name God as God." God knows who belongs to Him. Read it again! Carry it out on a silver platter to others! What kind of container will you become?

If we claim that we experience a shared life with him and continue to stumble around in the dark, we're obviously lying through our teeth—we're not living what we claim. But if we walk in the light, God himself being the light, we also experience a shared life with one another, as the sacrificed blood of Jesus, God's Son, purges all our sin.

1 John 1:6-7

Shared Life!

One of the great things about technology is the ability to share things instantly but even if it is shared instantly, the person who gets the invite must accept and open the information to receive it. I tried an experiment not too long ago where I shared a text with my family and buried a reward in the message of the text. I told them I would reward them if they responded to my message. The reward went unclaimed by my children. It was their choice and they had the opportunity but chose to not open it. I share files with my siblings on my parents' health and they have the opportunity to view the files just by clicking the link, but they do not. I share files with others who choose to respond or not. The choice is ours. If we claim we experience a shared life with Christ but never open His word or spend time listening to Him, we continue to stumble in the dark and it is obvious to all around us that we are lying. The shared life of light walking with God Himself as the light means we also share life with one another. If we are unkind, disrespectful, hurtful and mean to others, we are stumbling in the dark and there is no shared life light in us. When we walk in the light of life, our glow reflects on all around us. The dawn of a day pushes dark away and reflects on every surface as in this beach picture. As long as there is light, there is hope. Jesus is the Light of the shared life but we must open the door of the shared life and let the Light into our lives. We cannot continue to stumble around in the dark, proclaiming we have shared light when it is obvious we do not. What kind of light are you sharing? Are you opening the shared light life given to you by Jesus? Are you walking in it? Sharing it? Or are you lying through your teeth and pretending to walk in it while stumbling in the dark? What light are you shining?

That's exactly what Jesus did. He didn't make it easy for himself by avoiding people's troubles, but waded right in and helped out. "I took on the troubles of the troubled," is the way Scripture puts it. Even if it was written in Scripture long ago, you can be sure it's written for us. God wants the combination of his steady, constant calling and warm, personal counsel in Scripture to come to characterize us, keeping us alert for whatever he will do next. May our dependably steady and warmly personal God develop maturity in you so that you get along with each other as well as Jesus gets along with us all. Then we'll be a choir—not our voices only, but our very lives singing in harmony in a stunning anthem to the God and Father of our Master Jesus!

Roman 15:3-6

Combined Character!

Dependably steady and warmly personal are the combined characteristics of God in this passage. He says that God wants a combination of His steady, constant calling and His warm personal counsel in Scripture to come to characterize us to be alert for whatever He is doing next. I wonder what would happen if I truly and fully focused on building the character of God in my life rather than worrying about my personal needs and wants. Maturity is the mark of having accomplished a goal in growth's path. God desires spiritual maturity from each of us so that we walk in harmony with one another such that as we abide together, it seems as if a choir is performing a stunning anthem to God. Paul said Jesus waded right into our troubles and helped us out. He didn't try to keep Himself from having trouble but rather He took on our trouble for Himself so that we could see and understand this personal God. He wants us all to develop and mature in Him and in our walk. What is your combined character? More Him or more you?

Nothing and no one is holy like God,
no rock mountain like our God.
Don't dare talk pretentiously—
not a word of boasting, ever!
For God knows what's going on.
He takes the measure of everything that
happens. The weapons of the strong are
smashed to pieces, while the weak are infused
with fresh strength. The well-fed are out
begging in the streets for crusts,
while the hungry are getting second helpings.
The barren woman has a houseful of children,
while the mother of many is bereft.

1 Samuel 2:2-5

God Measure!

Perfect in goodness, sacred, pure, and set apart are all definitions of Holy. The book of Samuel says nothing and no one is holy like God. Then it adds there is no rock mountain like our God. It seems out of sync until you continue reading and you see the context. This is the dedication prayer of Hannah as she left her son, Samuel, to be raised in the temple of God. Hannah had yearned for a child but was barren. She promised God to give her child to Him in service if He would allow her to have one. Samuel was born and Hannah followed through on her promise. Hannah bore other children after Samuel but he was her firstborn and until his birth, she was barren. Culturally that was a very negative thing which left her alone and uncared for, made fun of and lonely. She grieved before God and God heard her. I know many friends who have been blessed with children after a long journey of barrenness and I know some who still struggle. There is a sense of worth inside us that is tied to the ability to bear a child whether we like it or not. It hurts when we desire a baby and cannot have one. I understand this pain as I struggled with child loss and God finally blessed us with our boys. I get this. I understand Hannah's heart. As she prayed, she prophesied also because her son would see the days ahead of pretense and how God displaced the pretentious for the humble. Weapons made of mortal hands are not those infused with strength. Holiness is the weapon of unbreakable bond. But not our holiness for we have none. It is His Holiness which we dwell in, live in, breathe and move in that has all the power to combat the weapons of the world. When we walk in weapons of our own warfare, we fail. When we walk in His Holiness, the weapons are infallible and unfaltering. Lay aside the weapons of your own making and take up the weapons of God. It is no wonder that it was a pebble that slew the giant when David took on the strength and Holiness of God. Whenever we try to operate in the flesh, we reap the things of flesh but to operate in truth, we reap the reward of Holiness. God takes the measure of everything that happens and He makes it right. Trust His measures because they are far more perfect and powerful than our resources and means. He makes all things right. Hannah knew this. She took her grief, desires and frustrations to Him and He used her to be the vessel of His calling as Samuel became a mighty prophet of God. What you are and what you do may not seem like much to you but in God's measure, He is doing mighty things for you and through you. Your one cup of oil is just a cup but His touch makes the measure a container of continuous outpouring. Just start pouring and trust Him to make it all it needs to be. Trust God's measure of Holiness.

So we're not giving up. How could we! Even though on the outside it often looks like things are falling apart on us, on the inside, where God is making new life, not a day goes by without his unfolding grace. These hard times are small potatoes compared to the coming good times, the lavish celebration prepared for us. There's far more here than meets the eye. The things we see now are here today, gone tomorrow. But the things we can't see now will last forever.

2 Corinthians 4:16-18

Small Potatoes!

Today is a celebration! An anniversary of an accomplishment here in my world. I am celebrating many years as a successful small business owner despite the struggles and hard times. I am celebrating with a fun celebration for all of my clients and staff for the past fifteen years because they deserve to be honored for being faithful to refer and commit to my business. But my celebration is small potatoes compared to the celebration that Christ Jesus is throwing for His bride at our homecoming. Some days, from the outside, it looks like things are completely falling apart. However, on the inside, where God is making new life, not a day goes by without His unfolding grace and mercy. The truth is that God's promise, like a rainbow, is always there. It simply takes the right circumstances for us to catch a glimpse of it. God's light is always around. Catching His light and refraction of it into the many colors in a rainbow happens in a lot of ways, but most commonly through water vapors in the air or clouds bending the light into prisms. Rainbows appear to come and go. Here today, gone tomorrow but the truth is that they are simply a reflection of His promise and His promise is forever. We look at the fleeting beauty of a rainbow and for the moment, we are reminded of His promises. But the things we cannot see, the promises, are forever. Your life may feel as if it is falling apart, but know this, His promises are still strong and true. Do not let the things that appear to be falling apart and fading like the rainbow, disconnect you from the promise. The promise is just behind the cloud. It is waiting on you to refract and reflect His love. The rainbow of His promises is within you. You simply have to latch onto the eternal and begin to refract His promises from the inside to the outside so they can shine beyond the clouds like the colors in this sunset. Celebrate Jesus! Celebrate His goodness, His life, and His promises! Celebrate Life everlasting despite the trials! Find the beauty in the simple and refract His love onto others so they too might see His goodness and mercy. Today is a day of celebrating the small potatoes because though they feel like mashed up dreams, I am planning to mix them with the milk of His word and enjoy some mashed potatoes while I await the glorious return of our Savior. Troublesome times and Lavish Celebrations both exist. We get to choose which mindset to live in. Pain only lasts for a while. Joy comes in the morning! Get busy making the best God has to offer with what He has given you. Quit whining and worrying! Start celebrating!

Every time the Animals gave glory and honor and thanks to the One Seated on the Throne—the age-after-age Living One—the Twenty-four Elders would fall prostrate before the One Seated on the Throne. They worshiped the age-after-age Living One. They threw their crowns at the foot of the Throne, chanting,

Worthy, O Master! Yes, our God!
Take the glory! the honor! the power!
You created it all;
It was created because you wanted it.

Revelation 4:9-11

Living One!

The four animals in Revelation that give the Glory, Honor and Thanks are a conglomeration of people in a country. The Revelation lists them as like a Lion, Eagle, Ox, and possibly a Monkey or such as it just says it had a human face. Every time the "Animals" worship, the Elders fall prostrate before God in worship. Worship here drives worship in Heaven. What you do matters. Your worship matters. Last night, I dreamed of animals, made of puzzle pieces of people, around the throne of God walking, flying, moving in worship. I saw these "animals" declaring the glory through the tough times and I saw the elders fall down in chorus as if a wave of extreme emotion and glory fell on them. They worshiped. Worship is the tide changing key to open prison doors. You feel imprisoned by your finances, health, struggles or straits...begin to worship...for it breaks down prison walls and sets captives free. Every time we worship, all of Heaven worships. Every time. This is why Heaven is a place of worship. I don't understand all of Revelation but I do understand that our worship drives the worship in Heaven. I do know that there is rejoicing in Heaven when one is saved, when one goes home, and always when we worship. God created it all in His way. He created the birds of the air and the beasts of the field as well as the fish in the sea. He created you and me. Why? Because He wanted to do so and because He longed for us to worship. Our worship, glory and honor to Him is the doorway to the floodgates of blessing. Not because we have to do it; not because it is the way to blessings; but because of who He is. I could equate animals to countries like the Eagle to the USA and the Oxen to the tribes of Israel and the Lion to the Netherlands and the Monkey to the South American countries or I could just quit trying to puzzle it out and be a piece of the worship. I can be the reason that there is worship for God on Earth and in Heaven. I can be the reason that His heart is turned towards us. I can be His hand extended. I can be a piece of pipe He uses to minister to others. I can be a part of the Revelation of who He Is. I can do all that by worshiping He who sits on the throne. My praise has power. My praise has meaning. My praise is the key to open the windows and doors of Heaven in my life. Worthy, O Master! Our God! Take all the glory, power, and honor for it is all Yours. You created it all for your glory. Simply let me be the source of worship. Allow me to be a vessel of your praise. I would rather be used of you, in honor and glory to you, than to have all the accolades of this Earth. I long for you, Lord. Let me be the reason that the Elders worship. Let me be the spark that ignites the blaze. Let me be the one who is willing to worship despite it all. You are worthy!

Don't fret or worry. Instead of worrying, pray. Let petitions and praises shape your worries into prayers, letting God know your concerns. Before you know it, a sense of God's wholeness, everything coming together for good, will come and settle you down. It's wonderful what happens when Christ displaces worry at the center of your life.
Philippians 4:6

Praise Shaped!

There is an old saying "shape up or ship out" which means to "get your act together" or "figure it out." This has been a motto in my life. All my life I have relied on my independent instincts to figure it out and when the road got rough, I learned to take it to God in prayer. I am "today years old" as the expression goes, when I finally grasped that this isn't how God wants us to do life. God doesn't want us working in the me time and coming to Him when the "me" ends or is worn out. He wants us to allow Him to shape us. One way He instructs us to allow Him to be the shaper of our destiny is for us to shape our worries into prayers. Shaping requires work on our part to actually capture those thoughts that lead us astray of Him then invite His presence into our worries through our praise. This photo is a rare occurrence of a hole of ice crystals shaped into the cloud likely by the passing of an airplane. It is a beautiful phenomenon that's rarely occurring on our planet but it happened by something that often occurs. Planes passing through clouds happens thousands of times daily but this shape happening and being caught on camera is rare. Prayers happen often, likely more often than planes passing through clouds, at least I hope so. God shaping our lives happens daily and often as we see it occurring. The rare occurrence is when we shape our worries into prayers such that the worry becomes praise. This is the foreground of miracles. When your worry becomes your praise, you have begun to walk on the waters of faith. The power of praise shapes your worries into prayers which brings miracles through faith because you allow God to know your concerns and when you praise Him, He bestows a sense of wholeness, peace and tranquility like no other. It's wonderful what happens when Christ displaces worry at the center of your life. God comes and shapes you, settles you and molds you into the place and person He desires you to be. All you have to do is begin to tell Him all about it first. Then allow Him to become the change that takes shape in your life.

"Count on it: Everyone who had it in for you will end up out in the cold– real losers. Those who worked against you will end up empty-handed– nothing to show for their lives. When you go out looking for your old adversaries you won't find them– Not a trace of your old enemies, not even a memory. That's right. Because I, your God, have a firm grip on you and I'm not letting go. I'm telling you, 'Don't panic. I'm right here to help you.'

Isaiah 41:11-13

Don't Panic!

As storm after storm has come into my life lately, I will admit that it has been easy to get overwhelmed and to start feeling anxiety. As I opened the Word this morning, it was like God knew! He always does. The first thing He addressed was those who have done us wrong. Sometimes it is hard to let things go when you feel you have been wronged. But He clearly says that those who have it in for us and work against us will end up as the real losers-out in the cold, empty-handed, nothing to show for their lives. But before you go celebrating this, you need to examine your own life and see if there is anyone you have done wrong because this could apply to you if you have not made the effort to make the wrong into a right by asking for forgiveness. God says He has a firm grip on us and He isn't letting go, so we are not to panic but to realize that He is right here to help us. Don't be discouraged or distracted by what seems to overwhelm you. Trust in Him and know that no matter what it looks like-those blessings are coming-maybe through raindrops-but they are coming! He is holding you and helping you even when you cannot feel it. Trust Him even when it seems hard. Hold fiercely onto His promises! Restate them. Post them! That is a reason I write each morning and put these screenshots with scripture. Print them or buy the book and read them daily. Just hold on! His promise: I, Your God, have a firm grip on you and I'm not letting go! Don't panic! I'm right here to help you! Say it again. Read it, claim it! Count on it!

We, though, are going to love–love and be loved. First we were loved, now we love. He loved us first.

1 John 4:19

First Love!

I am not sure what it is that makes love different person to person but it is. I used to get so irritated when my mom would tell me that I couldn't understand her love for me until I had my own child, then I had kids and I understand. I would watch older couples and think how sweet it was to see them with each other and now I understand. My friend told me there is such a unique love for a granddaughter, I do not yet have a grandchild but I do believe her, because I have seen it. My sons are both loved deeply but differently and I cannot explain it. It isn't less or more, it is a unique love. Mature love is a love that grows. The love of a mother has grown as she carries that child within her, placing hopes, dreams and the willingness to sacrifice her very life to give them life. Love isn't a simple emotion but a complex action of faith, hope and God. God is love. He loved us first because He created us. He infused us with His very breath. The first chapter of John is all about The Word of Love. Love is God and God is Love. They are synonymous. This first love cannot be replaced by a mortal love nor sex nor worldly lust nor power nor riches....nothing takes the place of first love. It is a God sized hole in our lives aching to be whole like a puzzle with the final piece missing until we step back into His love. If you are searching for answers, solutions and the way to be free; if you are longing to be loved and accepted, embraced and whole, step into His love. He says Here I Am. I love you with an everlasting love. Fullness, completeness, wholeness and contentment are all found in His love because He is your first love. Your longing is for Him. Your desire you cannot fill with social media nor friends nor parties nor anything else because your desire is for Him. He delights in you for He is your first love. He loved you first. Now we love. Tell Him, embrace Him through your words of praise and worship His name. His fullness of love is like no other and I can only tell you about it until you experience it. It is unique like no other. His love for you is yours alone. He waits for your embrace with open arms. Run to Him.

Nothing, you see, is impossible with God."

Luke 1:37

Attempt the Impossible!

(Sermon notes from messages by Pastor Ray Holman)

Matthew 14:27-33; Luke 1:37

Don't Listen, Lounge, Linger or Look Don't Listen to Your Detractors as there is always someone to tell you that your situation is impossible. You need to speak to people who will encourage and speak the word over you rather than what appears as "reality". Negative reports can be ingested, digested and walked in or they can be put into the hands of The Great Physician. Don't Linger in Your Own Strength. Your strength will forever let you down. His strength is perfect in your weakness. Attempt something so great that without God it is impossible. Walk in the "what if it does" instead of the "what if it doesn't". Don't let your situation determine your destiny. Will your faith allow you to get out of the boat? Ask in Faith then Act on that Faith. If you will run and shout for the miracle when it happens, then be willing to run and shout before the miracle, for the miracle. You need to prepare for the storms ahead spiritually before they come as we know they are coming. Don't Lounge in Your boat in the midst of the Storm. Do not let Fear keep you from stepping out. Do not let your own doubt keep you from stepping out into the miracle. Walking on the water will not happen if you never step out towards God. The bold step of faith out of the safe place into the storms of life starts with going to Jesus. Every miracle of life starts with a bold step of faith. They are not for show. They are so others can see the power of God evident in our lives. Stepping into God's purpose is often the place of the impossible. James 2:17. Action is the life of Faith. Doing the impossible for God will never happen unless we are willing to get out of the boat. Walking on water cannot happen until we trust Him enough to get out of the boat. Don't Look at Your Circumstances or the Waves or the Impossible but look at the Savior instead. If Jesus is the WayMaker, then look to Him instead of your situation.

Matthew 14:31

Peter crawled out of the boat in Faith but then doubt and fear got ahold of him as the noise of the storm and the waves got ahold of him. The circumstances seem overwhelmingly impossible but at that point you must fix your vision on Jesus Christ not on anything else. 2 Corinthians 5:7 You gotta keep walking by faith not by sight. If you walk by sight alone, then you'll never be able to do the impossible through God. When you lose sight of Jesus, you lose your sense of purpose and your identity. Find God in the midst of the circumstances rather than trying to figure it out. In the midst of everything, shut it down and start praying. James 1:6 When Jesus grabs Peter, He walks with him through the storm. He didn't cease the storm. He took him through the storm. The circumstances caused fear/doubt/sinking but when Jesus took him by the hand, his confidence was restored to walk through the storm. When they got to the boat, Jesus asked, Why did he doubt and stated he was of little faith.

Hebrews 12:2

Living in the realm of the impossible with God is harder than it seems. It is easy to see the waves and feel them, but God is still there.

He told them, "You don't get to know the time. Timing is the Father's business. What you'll get is the Holy Spirit. And when the Holy Spirit comes on you, you will be able to be my witnesses in Jerusalem, all over Judea and Samaria, even to the ends of the world." These were his last words. As they watched, he was taken up and disappeared in a cloud. They stood there, staring into the empty sky. Suddenly two men appeared–in white robes! They said, "You Galileans!–why do you just stand here looking up at an empty sky? This very Jesus who was taken up from among you to heaven will come as certainly–and mysteriously–as he left."

Acts 1:7-11

Last Words!

Our last words are the things we hope we say right. Life has lots of twists and turns. Often, we do not know when our last words to a particular person will be spoken so it is important to take care. My friend/colleague who is a Life Strategist, Radio Host and LPC asks the question every day as he signs off his show: "If today was your last day on Earth, who would you call, what would you do, what would you say? Why are you waiting? Make the Call!" Our last words to each person every day could be our last words to them forever. Ever thought of that while you are busy being ugly? I have a neighbor at my business park who is not nice at all. The sad thing is that were she not such a mean person, she would be pretty. Her attitude and approach to everyone she meets is spiteful and hateful. She curses, derides, mocks and screams. I feel so sorry for her. All of my clients know her because she acts like this daily, so often that she is called the crazy lady. She doesn't care who she screams or curses at. She just has a mean spirit. What makes her so upset? People driving or parking in the parking lot on the side she perceives is hers. There are plenty of spaces. It would make her business look prosperous but instead she spends her days watching out the window waiting to come scream at someone. Such a sad thing because most of the time, those are her last words to people who could be her potential clients but they will never use her services because of her words. Each day we have the opportunity to make an impact on the people in our realm of influence. We can become someone else through our actions, words, and deeds when we are upset, so we must remember, what if these words, these actions, these moments were the very last impressions I made on this person. First impressions matter and last impressions matter. Sometimes, your first impression is the last impression. That person you are dealing with who is causing you grief may be going through unknown pain themselves. Try to be the person you would want God to be to you. Pray for His guidance. You see, His last words to His people before ascending to Heaven was to wait on the Holy Spirit, then when He comes to you, be a witness in everything and everywhere you go. What is the impression you are leaving behind you? Is it a lasting impression of who God is or is it a lasting impression of who you are? Do they see Jesus in You?

Plain Truth!
Luke 21:1-4

Giving all is the ultimate gift that Christ gave for us! What is all that God desires from us?

Is He our first, your priority above all else or is the time with Him the things that get sacrificed on the altar of self?

What would you do to spend time in an audience with The King? Why are you waiting?

Key thought for today:

The Best!
I Thessalonians 5:15

Giving the best of us is the challenge we must understand and undertake. What is your best? Are you giving it to Him?

Are you looking for the best in others? Are you doing your best to bring it out in them?

Key thought for today:

Royal Authority!
Luke 22:27-30

How does the two letter word, "As" have such great importance here in this scripture?

With authority comes responsibility which means:

We want things to happen, but first we have to take action. What is the mountain in the way of your ministry?

Key thought for today:

Mine Forever!
Psalms 119:105

We have all been given the best gift of all, but what we do with it is what really matters. What does this scripture in Psalms say about this gift?

How can we put into practice what we learn from Philippians 4:8-9?

Key thought for today;

Constant Calling!
Romans 15:4

God desires His warm, personal counsel and His steady, constant calling from His word to characterize our lives. What is the point being made in Romans 15:4?

What does it take for us to be aligned with God?

Key thought for today:

Coming Day!
Luke 23:26-31

Deadwood or Green tree? Are you alive in Him, allowing Him to flow through you no matter the circumstances or are you dead wood, just fodder waiting to be kindling in the fire?

Key thought for today:

Words Remembered!
Luke 24:4-8

We remember things that are unimportant and forget things we should remember. Why is it so important to hide God's word in our hearts?

Do you have a favorite scripture that is an encouragement to you in times of distress?

Key thought for today:

Steady Stream!
Matthew 4:4

If God turned to "The Word" in order to sustain himself, shouldn't that be our first choice? But, do we always do that? Why do you think that is?

Key thought for today:

God Breathed!
2 Timothy 3:16-17

Each of us has a God-Breathed purpose in us. Each unique for what God has designed us to be. What abilities/tasks do you believe God has given you and are you thriving in them? Why/Why not?

Key thought for today:

Serious Searching!
Jeremiah 29:13

What are you seeking that is more important than the God of the Universe who has promised you won't be disappointed in what He does for you if you will seek Him with all your heart?

Key thought for today:

Real Surprise!
Ephesians 3:8-10

Our purposes and our marketplace of ministry may look very different but He has called us and purposed us with yet unopened gifts to be used for His glory. What will you open in His presence today?

Key thought for today:

Image Making!
Amos 5:24

The call for judgment has been issued. Will we turn again to His oceans of love or will we be consumed by our image making selves? The choice is ours. He calls us in waves of love to abandon the pursuit of self and once again turn to our first love.

What are some areas in your life that you need to change in order to respond to God's call?

Key thought for today:

Supple Moves!
Luke 6:27-28

When we learn His moves and His harmony, we begin to move gracefully in the dance with the King. The key is to exercise it. How will you embrace this challenge, change your perspective and become more flexible?

Key thought for today:

Fits & Starts!
Ephesians 4:2

As Paul sat in prison, he sent a letter to the church to not become a place of fits and starts but to be purposeful in the journey towards God.
Are you steadily walking and running or are you getting distracted by other things that do not truly matter to the final destination?

Who are you carrying or stopping to help along in this busy journey of life?

Key thought for today:

Recognizing Him!
Luke 24:28-31

We fail to recognize Him in our lives in our daily tasks because we are consumed with our day to day so that we fail to accept the possibility of Him living and breathing in us and through us in the minute by minute.

 As we walk along in life with others, who are they seeing? Are they seeing Jesus in us or are we so busy with self that He is shoved aside unseen? What do our mannerisms and actions tell others about who He is in us?

Key thought for today:

Prevailing Purpose!
Proverbs 19:21

God's purpose and plans prevail no matter what and when we align in His way, we will not fail. Have you been trying to do everything your own way? Why not yield to his purpose and plan?

Key thought for today:

Deep Spirited!
Philippians 2:3

Deep-spirited means being in _____ through the tough times and not being an _____ person.

His example to us was just this: He will _____ all our needs if we will but trust and do for others _____.

Man failed God but God in His _____ for His creation, gave _____ as an atonement for the law to redeem that old covenant into newness through His perfect _____.

Will you give something you love or cherish of great value to another In sacrifice to demonstrate His love?

Key thought for today:

Gods Terms!
Romans 8:11

Life on God's terms means: _____
_____.

The Spirit of God that raised Christ from the dead dwells in us when we _____
_____.

Accepting God's terms means accepting that He gave all for us so that we might give freely of ourselves to Him.
His terms are life, _____. His terms are _____,
_____ and _____. His terms are above all _____, _____ and
_____. Today is the day to begin to declare the victory of His terms and walk in Him!

Key thought for today:

Flowing Down!
Psalms 133:1

God is calling His people to a place of agreement in Him.

When we are contending with one another, He will not bless that place until we are in harmony with Him. This does not mean we have to agree on all things but it does mean we must set our eyes and heart on Him. What would our world look like if we were pulling together and helping one another?

Key thought for today:

The Focus!
Philippians 4:8

What are the things God wants us to focus on?

If we focus on these things and meditate on them constantly, then we reach the sum total of who HE is-the pure light, pure love, perfect God. So, what are you focusing on?

Key thought for today:

God Conviction!
James 2:14-17

What is God conviction?

What are God acts?

Why can we not just speak the words without taking any action on our part?

Key thought for today:

Particular Please!
Hebrews 13:16

Simple everyday tasks like washing dishes can become a gift of praise to God just by your mindset. What things are ahead for you today?

Mindset matters. How can we experience God's particular pleasures?

What can you do today to be His hand extended to others?

Key thought for today:

Healed Inside!
James 5:13

Why are we so eager to accept His death as atonement for our sin and His resurrection as proof of eternal life but we are not so open to accepting His stripes for our healing?

Do you believe that a lack of faith causes lack of healing?

Key thought for today:

Life-Light!
John 1:5

Who is our eternally present Life-Light?

Are you facing a situation that seems to have no way out?

Are you staying plugged in to the source of hope and encouragement? Continue to give Him praise and look for that glimmer of Light!

Key thought for today:

Back Right!
Psalms 103:13

We have a compassionate and caring Father, who loves us. In this passage how does David describe His love?

Does this hold true for you when you are needing a place of rest?

Key thought for today:

Grace Shower!
Ephesians 2:10

The word shower means to rain down upon. In this passage Paul is relating that God in His grace has made us alive through Christ Jesus, What is it that we are/were created to do?

Are we to do this alone?

Key thought for today:

Recover Life!
Matthew 11:28

In this passage we are told that we can come to God and He will give us rest from our burdens. What have you been trying to carry on your own? Isn't it time to give it to Him and let Him show you the way?

Key thought for today:

Full Measure!
2 Corinthians 1:3-4

Is there someone you care about who has a heavy burden? Won't you take time to let them know you care? What are some ways you can do that?

The believing had to overcome the naysayers by doing what?

How does praise bring down the walls?

Key thought for today:

The Best!
John 2:9-10

Often we get overwhelmed in our circumstances and we need someone else to stand in the gap, say the prayer, believe in faith and even be there through our circumstances. Can you relate a time this happened for you?

What is the action that brings about the Best? What is the most important thing we can do?

Key thought for today:

Trustworthy!
John 2:23-25

Do you consider yourself trustworthy?

Would Jesus see you as trustworthy with His life?

What are you doing about Jesus?

Do people see Jesus in you?

Key thought for today:

God Absorbed!
Romans 8:6

Are you allowing yourself to be fully cleansed by soaking in The Living Water and power of the Word?

What happens when we allow ourselves to take in too much of the world around us?

Is it time for a soaking, cleansing renewal of His Spirit in you?

Key thought for today:

Listening Truth!
John 3:5-6

Submission to the _____ over the flesh is the key to the _____.

What truth are you listening to? Jesus says He is the Truth, The Way and the Life and no man comes to the Father but through Him. Are you listening?

Unless a person _____ their life completely to this original creation-the spirit-then they miss the point of existence.

Key thought for today:

Redoubled Effort!
Philippians 2:13

Paul instructed the Philippians and us through the Word to be energized in our life of salvation and to be reverent and sensitive before God.
Having the energy of God means _____.
When it looks impossible, remember He is _____.

What impossibility are you looking for the God of the impossible to see you through?

Key thought for today:

Perfect Love!
1 John 4:11-12

What is love?

Are you feeling stretched today, thank God because He is preparing you to love more. Will you choose love? Will you choose God? Will you choose this day to serve?

Key thought for today:

Proper Behavior!
Ephesians 5:1

His love is....

How do we love like God?

Key thought for today:

Testing Challenge!
James 1:12

Count your blessings, Can you name just a few?

What is the reward for those who persist in loyal love of God through the testing challenges of life?

Key thought for today:

Wordless Sighs!
Romans 8:28

Are you tired of waiting? Let it all go....

Key thought for today:

Happy Life!
Psalms 105:1

Where is true happiness found?

What are you thankful for today?

Key thought for today:

Reach Out!
Ephesians 3:16

Are you ready to explore the extravagant dimensions of God's love?

Will you choose happiness in your circumstances and experience His infinite love?

Key thought for today:

Right Here!
Romans 10:9

We allow our emotions to dictate the truth rather than simple trust. Why?

What is a lack of faith? Do you really trust Him?

Take this situation Lord....

Key thought for today:

Wholly Mature!
John 15:12

What is wholly mature joy?

Will you choose Joy?

Key thought for today:

Catch His Breath!
Psalms 34:18

Have you or someone in your life been "gut punched"? Won't you lean in and Catch His Breath? Breathe Him in....

Key thought for today:

Urgent Job!
Acts 20:24

Are you feeling the urgency?

If you knew today was the day, who would you tell? Why are you waiting?

Key thought for today:

Strong Warrior!
Zephaniah 3:16-17

What promise is given here for us?

Are you ready to walk into his strong arms of love?

Key thought for today:

Talking Praise!
Psalms 100:4

Will you choose to walk in His truthful light of praise that casts a rainbow of promise through your storms?

Start with thanking Him right now!

Key thought for today:

God Container!
2 Timothy 2:20-21

What kind of container are you?

Are you willing to dive into His word and become the servant of the Almighty to carry the fine meals to others or are you simply comfortable being the compost heap receiving only the morsels and repeating those to others?

Key thought for today:

Shared Life!
1 John 1:7

What kind of light are you sharing? Are you opening the shared light life given to you by Jesus? Are you walking in it? Sharing it? Or are you lying through your teeth and pretending to walk in it while stumbling in the dark? What light are you shining?

Key thought for today:

Combined Character!
Romans 15:5

What is your combined character? More Him or more you?

What would happen if you truly and fully focused on building the character of God in your life rather than worrying about your personal needs and wants?

Key thought for today:

God Measure!
1 Samuel 2:2-5

Define Holy:

Will you lay aside the weapons of your own making and take up the weapons of God? Or will you continue to operate in the flesh, reaping the things of the flesh?

Key thought for today:

Small Potatoes!
2 Corinthians 4:18

God's promise, like a rainbow, is always there. It simply takes the right circumstances for us to catch a glimpse of it. We get to choose which mindset to live in. Which will you choose?

Key thought for today:

Living One!
Revelation 4:11

Why did God create you and me?

What does our worship do here on earth and in heaven?

Key thought for today:

Praise Shaped!
Philippians 4:6

What does God want us to do with our "worries"?

When your worry becomes your _____, then you begin walking in _____. Won't you tell Him all about it?

Key thought for today:

Dont Panic!
Isaiah 41:13

When you belong to God there is no reason to fear, So why do we allow our circumstances to put us in a panic?

What are some promises God has given to you? Say them, read them, claim them, then count on Him, he will come through!

Key thought for today:

First Love!
1 John 4;19

Love isn't a simple _____ but a complex action of _____, _____ and _____.
Who is our first love? Why?

Key thought for today:

Attempt the Impossible!
Luke 1:37

Don't Listen to Your Detractors. Who should we be listening to?

Don't Linger in Your Own Strength. Will your faith allow you to get out of the boat?

Don't Lounge in Your boat in the midst of the Storm. Will you allow fear to keep you from stepping out?

Don't Look at Your Circumstances or the Waves. Will you look to Jesus and allow Him to walk you through the storm?

Key thought for today:

Last Words!
Acts 1:7-11

What is the impression you are leaving behind you? Is it a lasting impression of who God is or is it a lasting impression of who you are? Do they see Jesus in You?

Key thought for today:

www.ingramcontent.com/pod-product-compliance
Lightning Source LLC
Chambersburg PA
CBRC090843120626
46551CB00009B/738